"In *Bless Your Husband*, Angela Mills has given us a treasure chest full of biblical truth, honest encouragement, and practical tips for investing in our marriages. Whether you are a bride-to-be or celebrating your golden wedding anniversary—or anywhere in between—you'll find countless ideas and inspiration in this book."

—Teri Lynne Underwood, author of *Praying for Girls: Asking God for the Things They Need Most*

BLESS
YOUR
HUSBAND

Published by Bethany House Publishers
11400 Hampshire Avenue South
Bloomington, Minnesota 55438
www.bethanyhouse.com

Bethany House Publishers is a division of
Baker Publishing Group, Grand Rapids, Michigan

Printed in the United States of America

ISBN 978-0-7642-3176-6

Library of Congress Control Number: 2018935313

Unless otherwise indicated, Scripture quotations are from the Holy Bible, New International Version®. NIV®. Copyright © 1973, 1978, 1984, 2011 by Biblica, Inc.™ Used by permission of Zondervan. All rights reserved worldwide. www.zondervan.com

Scripture quotations labeled BSB are from the Berean Study Bible (BSB) © 2016 by Bible Hub and Berean.Bible. Used by permission. All rights reserved.

Scripture quotations labeled NLT are from the *Holy Bible*, New Living Translation, copyright © 1996, 2004, 2015 by Tyndale House Foundation. Used by permission of Tyndale House Publishers, Inc., Carol Stream, Illinois 60188. All rights reserved

Cover design by Brand Navigation

Author is represented by Books & Such Literary Agency.

18 19 20 21 22 23 24   7 6 5 4 3 2 1

For Eric,
who persevered through those early years
with his fiery little flight risk of a wife
and loved her endlessly.

Contents

Foreword

I love a good road trip with my husband, Bill. For us, there is a sense of adventure and romance to piling in our car—or even better, in a rented sports car or convertible—and hitting the open road. We always have a destination in mind, but the journey is invariably a mix of spontaneous carpe diem moments of "seizing the day" blended with some strategic, researched, quixotic, and starry-eyed quests for the ultimate romantic experience. My husband and I map out treks to breathtaking vistas and go out of our way for these magical memories. Standing in these panoramic landscapes, we feel like the stars in our own love story. Wrapped in each other's arms overlooking a beautiful valley, sitting in a meadow of wildflowers, ankle-deep in waves lapping the ocean's sandy edge, kissing under the rushing cascade of a tropic waterfall—yes, these are the precious heart-to-heart, body-to-body thrills that invite romance in to break up the endless days of the very hard work of balancing career, kids, and community.

This book is like that kind of enchanted romantic tour.

But even more, this book is packed with the little things, the simple gestures, the small kindnesses that make every day, even the most ordinary day, a lovely, dreamy expedition to the heart of your man! And because this book is laid out as a series of very doable blessings aimed at fostering connection, unity, and intimacy, let's pause for a moment on one of those roadside vistas—from the vantage point of the heavenlies.

God values your love! The Creator connected you and your mate. No matter the circumstances, or how your relationship feels at this present moment, God created marriage and it is a reflection of God's love to the world. Your love is a light reflecting God's love. Therefore, you and your husband and the well-being of your relationship is carried on the heart and mind of God. He sees. He knows. He hears. He cares. And the loving Father, who created love, can help create love in your life and in your marriage too!

On our wedding gifts to each other, more than thirty-eight years ago, a verse was inscribed:

"We love because He [God] first loved us" (1 John 4:19).

God will love you two as well. And some of those lavish blessings to your love life will come through the blessings charted on the pages of this book.

In one of our books, I explain that "to bless means to speak well of another person" or "to provide with power for success or prosperity."[1] Angela's gift of *Bless Your Husband: Creative Ways to Encourage and Love Your Man* will give you tools, skills, ideas, and creative ways to bless your husband. It is like a roadmap, a GPS, for your journey of love.

Remember my love for taking detours to discover or create awe-inspiring experiences? Well, let me share how God led me to be writing the foreword for this wonderfully delightful and practical book. Very late one evening, I was working on a book proposal for my forty-sixth book. (You might be familiar with some of the books by my husband and me such as *Men Are Like Waffles, Women Are Like Spaghetti* and *Red Hot Monogamy*, or my books for wives like *52 Ways to Wow Your Husband* or *Red Hot Romance Tips for Women*.) As I was writing, my inbox alerted me to an email penned by a dear friend in publishing; she and another mutual friend at Angela's publisher were talking and planning for this amazing book you have in your hand right now, and they thought God might be calling me to be a part of this very important project.

I immediately signed up for the *Bless Your Husband* Facebook group. Then I began *doing* the blessing challenges and prayers. I facilitate a group called Red Hot Wife Challenge so I am a kindred heart with Angela and her desire to encourage and equip women to become more loving, caring, and engaged wives, but to my delight, I found it enjoyable and exciting to be on the receiving side of all of Angela's brilliant ideas. (And you will too!) I just *knew* I needed to *meet*, in person, this wife who seemed just as committed, called, and concerned about the well-being of wives and the creative power love can have to build strength into a husband's life. I admit it—I did a quick Internet search to discover that she lives in my state! Bill and I travel more than half the year doing marriage and family speaking, and as I glanced at my own schedule I saw that Bill and I would be within a thirty-minute drive of Angela's hometown. I messaged her to see if we could meet for a double date. It was a detour to destiny!

The double date was one of those "vista" moments. Our turn off the beaten path led Bill and me to a cozy coffee shop, with sweet treats and a terrific time of fellowship with Angela and her husband, Eric. We recounted our love stories, shared the ups and downs of our marriage treks, and we all agreed that God's faithful love can carry a couple through anything!

And that is my prayer for you, my fellow traveling companion, that God will carry you—and your husband—through whatever twists and turns the road of life is bringing your way today. I am convinced this book, *Bless Your Husband,* is your travel guide to marital coziness, unity, and intimacy. I am elated that you also have the opportunity to traverse this blessing challenge in a community of uplifting friends. I encourage you to gather your own friends, the women of your women's ministry, your Bible study, the wives in your family or workplace, and cheer each other forward in this high calling of being a loving wife and helpmate. If you are able, buy copies of this book as gifts and bless other wives in your friendship circle.

Successful love is simply a series of wise and healthy choices to bless. In my book *7 Simple Skills for Every Woman*, I share one of my favorite verses:

"Love each other deeply [fervently], from the heart" (1 Peter 1:22).

The word translated as *fervently* indicates stretching out, reaching—perhaps out of our comfort zones—to bless and build our husbands.[2] To love fervently is to love enthusiastically, eagerly, energetically, and intently!

Angela has given her best on the pages of this book; now it is your turn. Give your whole heart to this treatise of love. Decide to give your finest effort, your prioritized energies, and your thoughtful prayers daily to this adventurous journey to *Bless Your Husband.*

Your husband will be so happy that you are choosing to nestle up next to him on this road trip of wedded bliss—but you will also be the recipient of the blessing. There is never a downside to becoming your best self, a more loving person. All your relationships will grow and be enriched as a side benefit. And God promises to bless you too; somehow, someway, God will send a personalized blessing to enrich your life:

"[She who] refreshes others will be refreshed" (Proverbs 11:25).

Are you ready for this fabulous, fun, and fulfilling excursion toward a more loving marriage?

Simply turn the page—blessings, simple and sensational, are right around the bend.

Pam Farrel,
international speaker, author of forty-five books including
the bestselling *Men Are Like Waffles, Women Are Like Spaghetti,*
and co-director of Love-Wise, www.Love-Wise.com

Introduction

How to Use This Book

This book is for all kinds of wives. Wives who are just making it through the busy days—nothing wrong in their marriage, but nothing special about it either. Wives who are in happy, fulfilling marriages and want to do something extra to bless their husband and grow in the Lord. Wives who are in a rough spot and wonder if they will still *be* married by this time next year.

This book is for working wives who will do the daily readings in the evening or in the early morning before leaving for work. It's for those who stay home with children and will read the challenges during nap time or while hiding in the bathroom. It's for newlyweds, for wives who have been married for years (or decades), and those who will tackle the challenges while their husbands pursue their favorite hobby.

It's for all of those wives and for everyone in between. Because what you each hold in common is the fact that you want to express love for your husband in words and in actions. Who among us knew it was going to be so hard to do and to be what we vowed on our wedding day? Who knew that love was going to be a choice we made over and over? Who could have imagined, while standing at the altar in a white dress that made us feel like a princess, that we would one day wear stained sweats and argue with our husbands over how to load the dishwasher? (Or is that just me?)

A comedian once said, "Married people, you're not really selling marriage. All we ever hear about is how hard it is."

I laughed when I heard this, because it is so true. It's kind of shocking when you first realize how hard it is, isn't it? And our society has all too easily accepted that marriages are going to fail. So when a wife picks up a book like this and commits to being a blessing in her husband's life, it gives me warm fuzzy feelings. We're in this together!

Now, a little about how this book works.

This is an interactive book, which means you are expected to write all over it!

Each week consists of five days of reading/activities and an optional Weekend Reflection. Day One is a little different from the others.

Day One

Each week begins with an introduction to the week's theme, followed by Day One activities. You'll fill in a simple, goal-focused statement—something specific to consider and work on throughout the week. (You'll have quick, daily reminders of your goal as well, and a weekly goal check-in with the Weekend Reflection.)

The weekly memory verse will also be introduced on Day One. Then you're on to the challenges.

Bless Your Husband Weekly Challenges

This is the fun part. Every week you'll find a variety of challenges designed to bless your husband. Each day, or as you are able to throughout the week, choose a challenge from the list.

I've tried to take into account the different types of people, personalities, and love languages, so the daily challenges reflect an array of tasks. Some are hands-on, some are more emotional, others are spiritual. All will help you grow as a wife and in turn, bless your husband.

Most challenges will have a shareable hashtag attached to them. If you are active on social media, and enjoy connecting with others, you can share a photo or a post (while being sure to protect your husband's privacy) and use the challenge hashtag. Each hashtag starts with "byh" so it will be easier to find others who are following the challenges in this book. Don't get caught up in feeling like you have to post every day. Just do it when the mood strikes, and connect with others who are on the same day you are, while spreading *Bless Your Husband* cheer!

And don't be afraid to go low-tech. If you don't have or don't want to use a smartphone, anytime this book says to text or send something to your husband, simply write a note instead. Or use email, if you like. Find the alternative you and your husband are comfortable with and do that.

Some challenges are simple and quick, and others take a little more time. Never feel like you have to complete one on any given day. I am the queen of rescheduling tasks to fit my schedule! I encourage you to do the same. The prayer, verse, and reading each day will do much to grow your heart toward blessing your husband. The challenges are a delightful bonus, so don't worry if you don't complete one. Give yourself grace and focus on what you have accomplished, not what you've skipped.

The beauty of this book is that you can keep it for years and go through it again and again.

Days Two through Five

Once you've made your way through Day One each week, you'll move on to the rest of the days, when you'll work through each of the following sections, spending in total about fifteen minutes:

Weekly Goal

Fill in a quick statement to remind you of your weekly goal.

Pray

A suggested guided prayer will focus on either your husband's needs or how you can grow as a wife. Where there are Scripture verses supporting the prayer, those are noted so you can look them up if you like.

Meditate

After prayer, you'll do a quick, one-minute exercise to help you store that week's memory verse in your heart. Meditating on God's Word is a sure way to grow in character.

Dwell

Each day, you'll complete a fill-in-the-blank statement about your husband that is intended to focus your mind on his good qualities. Some statements are simple, others are deep, and some are silly. But they all will help you to train your mind to think on what is excellent. Some will help you remember what makes your husband special, and others will just remind you of or teach you (ask if you don't know) some of his favorite things.

Don't skip this section, because at the end of your six-week journey, you'll have something like a love letter with all of those filled-in statements. It will be nice to look back on when you need those reminders.

Breathe

In this section, you'll sit back, relax, and read daily thoughts for all of us who have accepted the six-week challenge. You'll be inspired and encouraged.

Reflect

This section is a daily guided journaling to complete after you have done the daily task. You may want to start with this each day, reflecting on the previous day's task. Some questions dig a little deeper into the challenge of the day, and some will just be fun to answer and learn more about yourself.

Weekend Reflection

At the end of each week, you'll find a Weekend Reflection section, with questions to answer and a place to check in on the progress toward your goal. You can answer these questions in the space provided, or you can use them for discussion questions, if you plan to do this challenge with a group. (For more information on using *Bless Your Husband* in a group setting, see page 184.)

Does this seem like a lot to take on every day? Don't worry, once you start Day One, you'll see that it only takes about fifteen minutes to complete each day. Some day's challenges may be a little more time consuming, but the majority of them are things you can easily add to your day, even if it's hectic.

Please note, this is not intended to be a strict challenge, it is intended to be a grace-filled one. There is no commitment to sign or pledge to make. Some days, you won't get around to doing the reading. It happens. That's life. Just pick up the next day and keep moving forward. Eventually, you'll finish. Resist the temptation to turn this into a checklist that defines how good a wife you are, and instead focus on how you have been able to bless your husband.

Before You Start,
or How Expectations
Can Wreck Us

When a blessing challenge is presented to some women, they respond by asking, "What about me? Why can't my husband spend six weeks blessing me?"

I get it. Who wouldn't love to be spoiled for six weeks? This challenge is about changing our hearts, not about changing our husbands. And that's a good thing, because in case you haven't figured it out yet, the only person you can change is yourself.

Now is a good time to check out your expectations and motivations for undertaking this challenge. Examine your heart. The reasons you want to bless your husband are more important than any of the tasks you end up completing because they reveal your heart. And God is all about our hearts.

> The LORD doesn't see things the way you see them. People judge by outward appearance, but the LORD looks at the heart.
>
> 1 Samuel 16:7 NLT

Heart Check

Let's look at some motivations for doing this challenge that might not be the best.

1. **You want to change your husband.** As I have already pointed out, this won't work. Only God can change him. This is one of the hardest things to remember as a wife. No matter how many times I remind myself, I find myself thinking that something I do is going to change how my husband reacts to things. When you do something for the right reasons (which we'll get to in a minute), you're the one who ends up changed.

2. **You want other people to think you're a good wife.** This can be a subtle thing. You might not be overtly thinking you're trying to impress others, but in your heart, it's what you really want. I used to belong to a marriage small group, and each couple would choose one thing to work on every week. Then, at our meetings, we would talk about how our week went together. All the husbands would complain vehemently about their wives, except for Eric, my husband, who always spoke kindly and positively about me, focusing on the good changes we were making. (And believe me, that is more a testament to *his* character than it is to mine.)

   It wasn't long before I felt pressured to keep up the whole godly wife thing. I didn't want to let him down, and I sure didn't want him complaining about me like the other husbands did about their wives! I was so worried that I couldn't live up to being a good wife that I took my focus off what God was doing in my marriage. Instead of depending on Him to change my heart, I was depending on myself to be good enough. And we all know that doesn't last long.

   A few months later, I was at a marriage seminar and watched a video of a well-known pastor and his wife. They spent the whole video talking about their bad attitudes, arguments, ridiculous fights, and how they worked through them. I have to say it was one of the most freeing experiences of my life.

   Because I realized then that everyone has problems, and that when you admit your shortcomings, you can actually grow, and sometimes you can even help others. These days, I'm free from the pressure to appear the perfect wife and homemaker, and because of that, I have freedom to be me.

Trying to seem like a good wife really isn't going to be enough to keep you going and will only give you superficial results.

3. **You are hoping for reciprocation.** Maybe you want your husband to have a better attitude, or you want him to praise you and thank you profusely, or maybe you're hoping for an actual gift—jewelry, flowers, or something. This motivator is self-centered; doing something to receive something in return will always backfire on you. You may get your way for a while, but when you're looking to get something back for every good deed, soon nothing will seem quite good enough, and you'll be left with the same dissatisfaction you started with.

    Of course, we hope our husbands will notice, and we hope they will be thankful. But that can't be the only reason you do the challenge.

4. **You want to make your husband feel guilty.** Your heart is not in the right place if this is your motivation, even if you think it's going to be a catalyst for him to change. I think at times we've all harbored this hope on some level. We might not go into a situation hoping to make him feel guilty, but we might get pleasure from his feeling bad and think that it's going to cause him to see the error of his ways.

    Of course, if you're really steaming mad at him, you may just want him to feel guilty when he sees what an amazing wife you are.

    You can't go into the challenge for this reason either.

Now let's talk about good motivations for doing this challenge.

1. **You want to make your husband happy.** You desire to cheer him, help him, and bring joy to his days. Maybe he's in a

bad place right now, and you think this will encourage him. Nothing wrong with that!

2. **You want to be a better person.** We all need to grow, and this is a good way to be less selfish and concentrate on what you can do for your husband. Maybe you need a little help focusing on your marriage, and the challenge can serve that purpose.

3. **You love your husband.** This is definitely a good reason! Maybe everything is pretty good in your marriage, and you're overflowing with love and want to bless your husband, celebrate your love, and make him feel special. That's awesome!

4. **Because you love God.** This is the best motivation of all for doing this challenge, and will stand up to the daily ins and outs of marriage. God never changes. Your feelings of love for your husband can and will change on a daily basis. Your desire to improve will come and go. Your need to encourage him will wax and wane. Make the decision to do this because you love the Lord and you want to obey His Word *and* love your husband.

Know that when you make this decision you will be attacked by the enemy. For sure. He doesn't want your marriage to thrive. So things will be going along wonderfully, and then you'll get in an argument or one of the kids will be out of control. You'll have financial problems. In-law problems. Illness. Something. And suddenly, it won't be so easy anymore to stick with the challenge. Doing this because you love God will keep you strong when your feelings won't.

A Final Thought about Expectations

Though this challenge may be a big deal to you, your husband may not even notice. Especially if you are already an attentive wife. He might not think to thank you or acknowledge your efforts. And that's okay. The blessings you will reap in your marriage will be reward enough.

He might even notice you doing one of the tasks and have a bad attitude about it. He might complain or criticize you. If that happens, try to remember that this challenge is about changing *your* heart, not changing your husband.

The challenge is about purposefully setting aside a few minutes a day to focus on your husband and bless him. It is not about getting a new spouse in six weeks. Though your husband just might feel like *he* got a new spouse!

Decide now to see this challenge through, all six weeks of it, no matter how your husband reacts, and no matter how long it takes you to get through it. And I promise your efforts will not be wasted.

The Wife of His Youth

> May your fountain be blessed, and may you rejoice in the wife of your youth. A loving doe, a graceful deer—may her breasts satisfy you always, may you ever be intoxicated with her love.
>
> Proverbs 5:19

Twenty-one years ago, I was getting ready to go on a date with a very cute guy I really liked. I had a one-year-old, so I arranged for a relative to watch her. I took a long, hot bath and put a mud mask on my face. I spent plenty of time on my makeup and hair, aiming for the naturally pretty look that somehow takes more time than the made-up pretty look. I tried on no fewer than four outfits, and asked friends for their input before choosing the perfect dress. I slipped my feet into killer stilettos, knowing they'd be aching before I even stepped out the door. I sprayed perfume on and practiced my smile in the mirror.

We went to a golf range. Yes, I knew ahead of time that's what we were doing, but I still wanted to look cute rather than be comfy at that point, hence the killer shoes. On the green, he wrapped his arms around me and showed me how to putt. We talked non-stop, laughing and sharing life stories. At the end of the night, he brought me back to my apartment and kissed me good-night.

27

There was lots of swooning as I analyzed the date later on with my friends.

Fast-forward to last week. My husband (the very cute guy I really liked) and I had been rescheduling a date night for about a month. We finally had a night free and were determined to have our date, using a gift card we had for a nearby restaurant. I wasn't feeling great. Not sick, just tired and achy and blah. So when he texted me about our plans that night, I let him know that I would be very fine with staying home.

We quickly changed our plans to involve takeout and Netflix. We found out that the restaurant we had the gift card for had a to-go option, so we put an order in and he stopped on the way home from work. When he got home, I was wearing his pajamas because all of mine were in the laundry. We ate on the couch, watched Netflix, and fell asleep. I don't think we said more than ten words to each other.

As far as dates go, that one pretty much stunk. And I couldn't help feeling bad, later, that we had wasted our restaurant gift card on such a non-date. I remembered that date at the golf range and knew I needed to get back to at least a little of my dating self.

Am I going to wear stilettos to a golf range? Uh, no. But I could step it up a little and actually leave the house for our next date.

Think back to when you and your husband were first dating. Do you remember how much care you took with your appearance before a date? Remember how everything he said was brilliant, and how all of his quirks were adorable? How you jumped to his defense if your friends said anything remotely critical about him?

The more comfortable you get with someone, the more you show your true self to them. Of course, this is a good thing. We wouldn't want to have to be "on" with our husband for the rest of our lives.

Being comfortable with each other means you get to be yourself and not worry about impressing anyone. You get to take care of each other when you're sick. You get to have lazy nights on the couch and days where you never change out of your pj's—and that's okay.

But settling into a comfortable place can also be a negative thing if we get so comfortable that we stop trying to improve. Unfortunately, we often save our worst behavior and attitudes for those closest to us.

Check Your Comfort Level — Day One

Are You *Too* Comfortable? A Quiz

Answer (Y) yes or (N) no to each question below.

Y N 1. Have you stopped worrying about sinful behaviors? When we're in the beginning of a relationship, we tend to present our best selves. And while we still probably struggle with some sinful behaviors, we try harder to keep it under control. If you're regularly sinning and don't even care, that's a problem.

Y N 2. Do you have crabby attitudes more often than pleasant ones?

Y N 3. Is there little to no physical intimacy between you?

Y N 4. Do you spend more time getting ready to see girlfriends or others than you do for him?

Y N 5. Do you regularly eat, watch television, or go to bed separately? We all need our downtime, and sometime this includes time away from your husband. But if you're doing these things separately for no reason more often than not, you may be getting too comfortable.

Y N 6. Have you stopped kissing goodbye?

Y N 7. Have you stopped greeting each other after a day apart?

Y N 8. Have you stopped caring about hygiene routines? We don't need to look like a million bucks every day, but if you're regularly skipping showering, shaving, or brushing your teeth or hair for long stretches of time and don't think twice about it, that's not a good sign.

Y N 9. Have you forgotten your manners? You don't bother saying *please, thank you,* or *God bless you.* This answer counts double if you use your manners with everyone but him.

Y N 10. Do you leave the door open while using the bathroom?

If you answered yes to four or more questions, you may be getting too comfortable with your husband. Pay extra attention to the challenges this week and see how you can improve.

Our focus this week is going to be on recalling that wife of our youth and bringing those qualities back to life. Even if you've only been married a short while, there are likely some things you can bring back from the honeymoon phase.

Weekly Goal

This week, think back to when you and your husband were dating and how you have changed since then. Hopefully, you've both grown a bit, but chances are there are some areas you've become laid back about maintaining. I know I tended to be more affectionate and generally more positive when dating my husband than I am now. Men are encouraged to "always be captivated" by the wife of their youth (Proverbs 5:19 NLT), and we can help them along in this by striving to be as lovable as we can be.

What can we learn from our younger selves? Why not think of some of the ways you captivated your man in the beginning, and choose to work on just one of those behaviors or attitudes this week?

This week, I will attempt to be _____, in the way that I was when my husband and I were first dating.

Memory Verse

He who finds a wife finds what is good and receives favor from the LORD.

Proverbs 18:22

Write this week's memory verse on a sticky note or index card and post it on your bathroom mirror or somewhere you'll see it often.

Week One Challenges

1. Make a copy of the Gratitude List you fill out on Day Two and give it to your husband. #byhthankfulformyhusband

2. Re-create your first date. Can you visit the same place you went then, or go somewhere similar? On the way to your destination, reminisce about your first date and rekindle the feelings you had when you first saw your husband. #byhrecreatingourfirstdate

3. Listen to "Your Song" together. After dinner, or after the kids go to bed, play the song and dance around the kitchen. (Or if you're like me, don't wait for them to go to bed, just go ahead and gross your kids out. It's good for kids to see that their parents are in love, and that they have some major dance moves.) Or play the song in the car, on the way somewhere, and squeeze his leg or rub his neck. However you do it, add plenty of affection and physical touch and let the music take you back to when you first fell in love. #byhweekoneoursong

4. Initiate sex. If your husband is the one who usually gets things started in the bedroom, he most likely will be pleasantly

surprised if you're the one to start things tonight. If he's too tired, sick, or not in the mood, try not to take it personally and settle for a cuddling session instead. (We'll skip the hashtag on this one. We don't need to share *everything*.)

5. Bake your husband's favorite cookies. If you don't bake, or if you're short on time, use the slice-and-bake dough from the grocery store. Back when you were first married, you probably made his favorite treats more often, so the smell won't just be delicious, it'll be a happy memory, too. #byhhisfavoritecookies

6. Buy a gift that will remind your husband of your honeymoon or another special destination. I found some Jamaican coffee for my guy and it reminded him of our mornings on the patio of our honeymoon cottage in Jamaica. You could get him a coffee table book with photos of your honeymoon spot, a deck of cards reminiscent of a Vegas trip, an orchid if you went to Hawaii, a wheel of Brie like the one you had in France, a Mickey Mouse shirt from Disneyland . . . you get the idea. Don't be upset if you have to clue him in on the fact that you're referencing your honeymoon. In fact, you just might want to add a card that says, "I was thinking about our honeymoon today!" #byhhoneymoonreminders

7. Plan a game night. Pop some popcorn and play a favorite game. Have fun and try to forget the pressures of day-to-day life that you didn't have when you were dating! #byhgamenight

A Gratitude List

Day Two

*Today I will be more _____ in
this way: _____ .*

Pray

Ask God to help you to persevere during this six-week challenge, that your motivations would be pure, and that you would be transformed by the renewing of your mind as you choose to think on what is good.[1]

Meditate

As you look at your memory verse today, highlight or underline it in your Bible. Do you agree that when your husband found you, he found what is good? Well, God said he did, so it's true! You are already a blessing in your husband's life!

Dwell

The last time my husband made me smile was when

_____

_____

_____

Breathe

Just this morning, as I was working on this book, I asked my husband if he had any ideas for how I could bless him. His first answer was predictably a sexy one, and I laughed and said, "No, I mean for my book." He was washing dishes at the time so that I could spend a precious Saturday morning in my office, hard at the work of encouraging wives.

I started giving him examples of the little things I'd been striving to do for the last few years, though I'll admit, I had been slacking off on the whole blessing thing lately. Yep, we had fallen into a comfortable yet stagnant routine of just getting through the days.

This was reflected in his reactions to the ideas I shared. He started giving me doubtful looks as I reminded him of all the lovely things I do. Okay, used to do. After a minute, I got irritated and snapped, "Let's not make this about what a crummy wife I am." Fortunately, I heard myself in that moment and was humbled.

Here was my husband, elbow deep in suds and listening to me ramble about my marriage book ideas, and it took nothing more than a few looks from him for me to lose my patience. If I had been even a little focused on the fact that he was doing what is considered one of *my* chores, maybe I would have been a little kinder.

Mercifully, he was in a good mood, and we laughed at the irony in my snapping at him while writing my book for godly wives, and we continued our discussion. He even gave me a few ideas that you'll be reading about in the days to come. But on a deeper level, I knew that my impatience was rooted in the fact that I have felt like a crummy wife lately.

Not because I believe we have to always be doing things for our husbands to be good wives. I don't believe that at all. But because I know that when I am actively working on my marriage, acts of kindness just spill out of me, and I find myself blessing my husband as a result. I knew that I hadn't really paid attention to my marriage in the last few weeks and that it was time to get back on track.

Maybe you're feeling the same way today. Like me, you may be comfortable but stagnant. If so, rest assured that the next six weeks are going to change that.

Whether you're in a great place, a stagnant place, or a volatile place that seems like it can only have a crash ending, focusing on the good is always a great place to start.

Reflect

A wonderful way to bless your husband is to make up your mind to see the good in him. Today, fill in this Gratitude List. If you're in a difficult spot in your marriage, it may take some time to complete this list. It may also take some time if you're not quick to think when it comes to writing. If so, that's okay. Take your time, even if it's over a few days, and fill things in as you think of them.

I Am Thankful . . .

1. For my husband's _____.
2. That he makes me feel _____.
3. When he _____.
4. For how he takes care of _____.
5. For his words when _____.
6. For the gift of _____ that God has given him.
7. For his _____ sense of humor.
8. For the way he _____.
9. That he chooses to _____.
10. For his perfect _____.

How long did it take you to fill in your list? Whether it went quickly or slowly, do you think this is because of the wealth of your husband's admirable traits, a lack of them, or because of your own ability to identify them?

_____

_____

What qualities are you thankful for that *you* bring to your marriage?

_____

_____

_____

If you completed a challenge today, list it here:

_____

_____

Day Three

Your Song

Today I will be more _____
in this way: _____.

Pray

Pray for your husband to have a heart that praises God. Pray that he sees who God is and that he will sing songs of praise to God all of his life.[2]

Meditate

Read this week's verse twice out loud, then attempt to say it without looking.

Dwell

My dance moves would best be described as _____.

Breathe

One day, when my husband and I were dating, still in that googly-eyed, mushy phase, we were driving somewhere in his car when he said, "Hey, I have a song for you," and he put a CD in. (That's how long ago it was, way back in the days of compact discs.) A Bob Marley song played: "I Wanna Love You." My twenty-year-old self was giggly but appreciative. It quickly became "our song," yet when it came time to pick the song for the first dance at our wedding, Eric refused to have "I Wanna Love You."

"I'm not dancing to that in front of your dad and grandpa," he said. "It talks about wanting to have you in my bed!"

I honestly didn't care what the song said, because I was young, in love, and rather stubborn, but I understood his discomfort and thought it was pretty considerate of him to think of how my dad and grandpa might perceive it.

So we went with another song that I loved and listened to often: "I Love You for Sentimental Reasons," by Nat King Cole. Sweet, timeless, and wedding-appropriate. Our first dance was a lovely moment, but I still felt that "I Wanna Love You" was our true song. And when we arrived at a lush resort in Jamaica for our honeymoon, guess what song was playing in the speakers along the walkways? Yep, Bob Marley for the win. For this sentimental wife, it felt like one more sign that we were *meant to be.*

Music moves us in ways nothing else does. A song can bring up instant memories, passions, anger, tears, joy, that elusive nostalgia, and even smells. In fact, singing songs is one of my favorite ways to worship God because I feel that it ties my mind and heart together like nothing else.

Yes, music can invoke a strong response in us. It is why most couples have an "our song." Whether it's something you listened to while dating, the song playing when you had your first kiss, or the first song you danced to at your wedding, chances are you have a special song that's just yours.

Have you considered how using music throughout your day might help improve your mood, energize you, or soothe you? I like to use music to keep me motivated when working out, or to lift our spirits if we're having a dreary day. I often play instrumental or vintage French music in the background while we're cooking and eating dinner. And I love to blast music when I'm cleaning, since that's a job I don't enjoy, and fun music makes it go faster. I have great memories of doing chores to music as a child and pausing to stop and turn my mom's Beatles album over when one side was finished. (That was even *before* compact discs!)

I encourage you to think about how music might help your days, and don't forget "your song." Don't let it just be the soundtrack to your past, listen to it occasionally in the present, too, and remember the feelings that made you choose it as your special song.

Reflect

Write out the lyrics of your song here:

If you completed a challenge today, list it here:

_____

Initiating Intimacy	Day Four

Today I will be more _____ *in*
this way: _____.

Pray

Pray for your husband's purity. Pray that he will not be tempted beyond what he can bear and that God will help him to stay strong and make good choices. Pray that both his thoughts and his words will be pleasing in the Lord's sight.[3]

Meditate

Copy this week's memory verse here:

_____

_____

Dwell

I find it incredibly sexy when my husband

_____

_____

Breathe

> Do not deprive each other of sexual relations, unless you both agree
> to refrain from sexual intimacy for a limited time so you can give
> yourselves more completely to prayer. Afterward, you should come
> together again so that Satan won't be able to tempt you because
> of your lack of self-control.

1 Corinthians 7:5 NLT

Sex is important. And it's not just your husband who thinks so;
the Bible makes it very clear, too. Regular sex keeps both husband
and wife from being tempted beyond what they can bear.

It was created by God as an act of love between husband and
wife, and it's like no other connection you will ever have with your
husband. And you're the only one who gets to have that connection
with him. Besides that, it's fun!

Yes, there are situations in which one partner can't have sex as
often as the other may like, for physical or even emotional reasons.
And no, not having regular sex is never an excuse for infidelity.

But sex *should* be something that happens regularly if it is
at all possible. There are a few good reasons to avoid or put off
having sex. A few examples include: doctor's orders, fasting and
abstaining for biblical reasons, if one of you is sick or in pain, or
if you're separated due to work or deployment.

However, a lot of the reasons for avoiding or putting off sex
really aren't valid. Being tired isn't a good reason to go too long
without sex. If you're too tired to have sex with your husband,
something else needs to be cut from your life. Or maybe you can
find a different time of day for intimacy. There's no rule that says
you can only have sex at bedtime.

Having kids isn't a valid reason to avoid having sex. Even if
they've been hanging on you all day, and even if they sleep in your
room. Find a place, find a way. If your kids are the age where they
have to be supervised every second, then you're going to have to
make time for your husband when they are sleeping.

Busyness isn't a good reason to forego sex for long periods of time. If you're too busy for sex, you're too busy!

Obviously, we all have seasons in our lives when we're super busy, tired, working too much, have just given birth, have an ill family member, or for whatever reason can't summon the energy for one more thing at the end of the day. I get it, I really do. And there will be some days like that and even some weeks like that. But if you find that those weeks are happening regularly, or that the weeks are turning into months, you need to reevaluate your choices.

Is there something that can be dialed back or cut out completely to make more time for physical love with your husband? Are the things that seem too important to cut out more important than your marriage? Most likely they are not.

Today's challenge might be difficult for some of you, but I want you to try anyway. I'm going to urge you to be the one to initiate sex with your husband. If you're unsure of how to do this, taking your clothes off is always a good start. In many relationships—not all, but many—the husband is the one who wants sex, asks for sex, and gets sex started the majority of the time.

What a blessing it would be for him to know that he is needed, he is wanted, and he is desired! If being the one to get things started is nothing new for you, then you're already ahead of the game. Maybe tonight you can go above and beyond and try to be extra attentive to his needs.

Whatever happens, don't be afraid to pray about your sex life. Remember, God created sex, and He already knows our every thought. If you're anxious about things going well, lift it up to God beforehand.

Reflect

How often do you think qualifies as having regular sex?

_____

_____

How do you think your husband would answer that?

_____

_____

_____

_____

If you disagree, can you meet in the middle, keeping 1 Corinthians 7:5 in mind?

_____

_____

_____

_____

If you completed a challenge today, list it here:

_____

_____

Day Five   # Gift Giving

Today I will be more _____ _in this way:_ _____ .

Pray

Give thanks to God for the specific gifts He has given your husband. Pray that your husband will be able to use his gifts to strengthen the body of believers, and that God will continue to guide him in sharing his gifts with others.[4]

Meditate

Write this week's memory verse from memory:

_____

Dwell

The best gift my husband ever gave me was

_____

Breathe

Gift giving can wreck people. We've all heard about a couple fighting or breaking up on a holiday because gifts were forgotten, unappreciated, or just plain wrong. Of course, none of us has ever argued over gifts. Nope. No way.

Do you remember shopping for a Christmas or Valentine's Day gift for your husband back when he was your new boyfriend? You didn't know what he was going to get you, or if he was going to get you anything.

Maybe you even asked his friends or family how much you should spend. Because no one wants to be caught giving their boyfriend an expensive watch for Christmas when he bought you a pair of fuzzy socks. Not because you're worried about the money, but you find yourself thinking, *Goodness! Way to scare him off. Why didn't I just make him a photo album of what our future children will look like?*

Funny story, I actually bought my husband a ring for Christmas one year when we were dating. When my dad saw it on Christmas Day, he said to Eric, "Sheesh, man, take a hint," and Eric looked like he wanted to crawl under a rock. Can I just say for the billionth time that I wasn't trying to propose? I just thought it was a nice ring. Honest! So, yeah, I know all about going in the wrong direction with a gift. Way wrong. Humiliatingly wrong.

Let's move on.

Another way gifts can be uncomfortable is if you have some negative associations with the idea. If you grew up with someone who used gifts as a bargaining tool, a substitute for love, or for control, it might be hard for you to express your love this way for fear of trying to buy your husband's affection. Maybe it's hard for you to even receive gifts from your husband without getting suspicious. If that's you, I hope participating in the gift-giving challenge this week will help you see things in a new, healthier light.

Someone in our extended family isn't very emotionally expressive, but this person lavishes gifts on those they love. They are not trying to buy anyone off, it's a way of saying I love you that's easier for them than saying the words. Because of this, I've had to teach my daughters that not everyone is big on hugs and words, and that this particular person has shown their love for them in a different way.

It was hard to explain the difference between trying to buy someone with gifts and using gifts as a way to say, "I care about you." We finally decided that it all comes down to your heart's intention. If you're not expecting anything in return (such as favors, forgiveness, or control), but truly just want to bring a smile to your loved one's face, then your heart is in the right place.

So, as with the rest of these challenges, give freely, don't expect anything in return, and you're good to go.

Just as some people have a hard time giving gifts, others have a hard time receiving them. Resolve now to show plenty of grace if your husband's reaction to any gift is not what you expected.

And finally, be aware of your budgetary boundaries and respect them. It's going to be hard for your husband to be excited about something if he's worried about how much money you spent.

Above all else, remember, it's the intention of your heart that matters.

Reflect

What is the best gift you've ever received? Given?

_____

_____

I have an ongoing note in my phone with gift ideas for loved ones. Consider starting your own list, so that when birthdays and holidays come around, you're ready with a few ideas. Start here and write down three gift ideas for your husband.

_____

_____

_____

If you completed a challenge today, list it here:

_____

Weekend Reflection

What was your score on the Are You *Too* Comfortable? quiz?

_____

In which area can you improve the most?

_____

_____

How did writing out and seeing your husband's good qualities on Day Two make you feel?

_____

_____

Before writing your Gratitude List, when was the last time you told your husband about one of the things you're thankful for?

_____

_____

How do you use music to help in your everyday life?

_____

_____

Do you think it's awkward to pray about your sex life? How can you overcome that feeling?

_____

_____

_____

Weekly Goal Check-In

How did you do with being _____ ,
in the way that you were when you were dating?

_____

_____

What was your strongest moment this week in regard to your goal?

_____

_____

What was your weakest moment?

_____

_____

How do you think being aware of this will help you as you go forward?

_____

_____

_____

The Servant Wife

We were enjoying lunch when one of the women in our group of friends broke the news that her marriage was ending. Her husband had been having an affair and he was leaving her for the other woman. None of us knew what to say, except to tell her how sorry we were.

She began to open up, and told us that she'd suspected the affair for a while. She and her husband had been friends with this woman, and she had begun to feel as if something was going on between the two of them. My friend kept her suspicions to herself, blaming her feelings on petty jealousy and not wanting to believe it was true.

The moment of truth came when they were all at a family party together and this other woman did the unthinkable. The hosts announced that the buffet dinner was ready, and this woman, without thinking about it, got up and fixed my friend's husband a plate of food and handed it to him with a smug smile.

My friend was stunned, and she said the tension in the room was palpable. She felt everyone watching her for her reaction. She

47

didn't say anything in the moment, but later that evening, she and her husband had it out and he confessed everything.

I was a new wife when I heard this story, and I remember feeling shocked that the other woman had brazenly done this. I couldn't imagine how my friend must have felt. I tried to put myself in her situation, and I felt hot rage on her behalf. How dare her husband cheat on her, and how dare this woman rub it in her face, and in front of her whole family?

This story has had a lasting impact on me. Not because of the infidelity, as sad as that is, but because it showed me the almost sacredness of a wife serving her husband. Clearly, there was the underlying tension of an actual affair going on, but the fact that it was something as simple as someone else getting my friend's husband a plate of food that blew the lid off of everything? That is what really spoke to me.

I tried to imagine that a woman, besides a family member, could fix my husband a plate of food at a party and I wouldn't bat an eye, but I couldn't shake the feeling that it would bother me. Probably because I had heard this story. Or maybe because it is such a personal thing to do for your husband.

Of course, my husband has been served by other women over the years, but the only instances I can think of are when someone else was cooking or serving and passing plates to everyone. I can't remember a time that I sat as someone else jumped up to fix him a plate of food. And I can't think of a time when it would happen.

Maybe I sound really, really old-fashioned right now. But I'm okay with that. It's how I was raised.

I grew up with a very close extended family. We had a ton of family parties, and we were always getting together for one reason or another. In our family, the women served the men. It was the women who set the big tables that crowded my grandparents' living room, who filled the glasses with ice, and made the strong iced tea. It was the women who cooked and filled plates for the little kids, and often for their husbands, too.

The men did their part, putting away the tables and folding chairs after we ate so that we could have the living room back for visiting. Other than that, I mostly remember the men sitting and visiting while the women rushed around taking care of everything. Even we young girl cousins had the job of passing out food and helping set the table while our boy cousins mostly got out of it. We never questioned it, because that's how it had always been.

To this day, our family parties are still the same. The women serve. And to this day, it doesn't bother me.

We're going to be talking about serving our husbands this week, and believe me it has nothing to do with fixing his plate at a party. But when I thought about how I wanted to start this chapter, my friend's story came to mind. *In whatever way we're serving our husbands, we should approach it as an honor that belongs to his wife alone.*

But what if the idea of being a Servant Wife is grating on you as you read this?

What if you weren't raised to serve your husband at all and it goes against your nature to do so? What if you feel angry at the mere suggestion?

If this is you, please know that we are encouraged several times in the Bible to follow Jesus' examples of servant-like attitudes. We are also commanded to love one another more than ourselves. The world has taken the idea of the loving service of a wife toward her husband and made it seem demeaning. Maybe even your own family has taught you that to serve your husband is beneath you.

Fortunately, it doesn't matter how you were raised or what your natural instincts are. You can learn to love serving your husband.

We must simply make up our minds to do so.

It doesn't matter if serving a man goes against everything your mother taught you. It doesn't matter if you grew up with a houseful of maids and never had to lift a finger. If you choose to follow God's commands, you can become a servant-like wife. Don't worry, I'm not going to tell you that it's your job to wait on him hand and foot. And I'm not going to say that my family's tradition of the women serving the men is the gold standard. We are, however, going to address how to get help from your husband when you need it.

So how do you become a servant wife?

God tells us that obedience brings blessings (Luke 11:28). If we choose to lovingly serve our husbands, we may not enjoy it at first, and we may even feel irritated about it. But if we choose to focus on putting God's commands into action, we can transform how we think about things.

If you're struggling with the idea of serving your husband, pray and ask God to help you make up your mind to serve him cheerfully, and take your first step of action by choosing one of the weekly challenges.

Day One — Acknowledging Service

A helpful step in learning to serve graciously and cheerfully is to first realize and acknowledge how we are being served by those around us every day. This week's goal is designed to help us do that.

Weekly Goal

Every day, identify some way you've been served. Maybe it's a simple courtesy, like someone holding the door open for you, or the mail carrier delivering your mail. Or perhaps your husband brings you coffee or gives you his jacket when you're cold.

Acknowledge these small acts of kindness out loud to the other person whenever possible. Go beyond a simple "thanks" and let them know you really notice and appreciate it. If you're not able to express your thanks, just being aware of how others are being helpful to you will brighten your day and will give you ideas of how you can pay it forward and serve others.

For_____ days this week, I will take a moment to acknowledge those who serve me.

Memory Verse

A new command I give you: Love one another. As I have loved you, so you must love one another.

John 13:34

Write this week's memory verse on a sticky note or index card and post it on your bathroom mirror or somewhere you'll see it often.

Week Two Challenges

1. After reading Day Two, give your husband some hands-on foot love. First, tell him you want to give him a foot rub, which he may be more open to than if you say you just want to wash his feet. Start by cleaning his feet, using a tub of warm water and a washcloth. Then, after drying them, give him a nice foot massage. You can use simple lotion, coconut oil, or olive oil for a soothing experience. #byhhandsonblessing

2. Choose something from the Make His Day Easier List on Day Four and resolve to do it every day this week. #byhmakinghisdayeasier

3. Thank your husband for the practical ways he helps you. #byhthankfulforhim

4. Watch his favorite movie or television show with him. Sit next to him, snuggled up close or holding hands, and let go of any distractions. Try to experience what you're watching the way *he* likes to experience it. If he talks throughout

movies, chat along with him. If he prefers silence, keep quiet. When I give my husband his way in this, I'm serving him in a unique way that makes him feel loved. #byhmovienight

5. Do one of "his" chores. Does he usually take out the trash, wash the car, or dry the dishes? Give him a break and tackle one of his regular duties. Even better, smile while you're doing it. #byhservingmyguy

6. Ask him what his top ten dinners would be, and work them into your meal plan over the next few weeks. Add the ingredients to your grocery list and make it happen. If he usually does the cooking, take over for one night. #byhfavoritedinner

7. This weekend, or the next time your husband is home in the morning, bring him breakfast in bed. Get up before he does and make some of his favorite breakfast foods. If you don't cook, you can get pastries from the store and fry an egg to serve with them, or even buy some frozen breakfast sandwiches or toaster waffles. Or you can order delivery or make a quick pickup from a favorite restaurant. Put everything on a tray with a steaming hot cup of coffee or another drink he'll like, and wake him up with a smile. #byhbreakfast

Day Two — Serving Like Jesus

Today I was served by _____ *in this way:* _____

Pray

Pray that your husband will have a strong desire to serve the Lord and that God will also give him the will to act on it.[1]

Meditate

As you look at your memory verse today, highlight or underline the verse in your Bible. Circle any form of the word *love* in red.

Dwell

My husband's eyes are _____ .

Breathe

What would you do if you knew it was your last day on Earth?

If taken as an amusing question, this can be fun to ponder, especially if money were no object. Phrases like *bucket list* and *last meal* come to mind.

But if the question were a serious one, the answer would be quite different.

On the night of the Last Supper, Jesus knew that He was about to be taken away from His disciples and sentenced to a brutal death. John 13 says that because He knew His time was short, He wanted to show His followers the full extent of His love.

The way Jesus did this was by washing the disciples' feet. After a long day of walking in sandals along dusty roads, it was common for people to wash their feet before entering their home or to have them washed in someone else's home. It was considered one of the most demeaning jobs, and the lowest-ranking servant in the home would perform this task.

So we can understand when Peter balks at the idea of Jesus doing this humble chore. Peter says, "You shall never wash my feet." Jesus answers, "Unless I wash you, you have no part with me." Peter then gets on board. "Then, Lord, not just my feet but my hands and head as well!" (vv. 8–9).

I feel that Peter and I would get along well. He always seems just a little on the lovably bratty side, and he loves Jesus so much.

I relate to his hot temper and too-quick answers, and I appreciate that he seems like a man without pretense. He apparently says whatever pops into his mind, and I love him for it. Because as quick as he is to hotly protest something Jesus says, he is just as quick to feel remorse and declare his love for Jesus.

Yes, Peter and I have a lot in common, so I shouldn't be surprised that when someone wanted to wash my feet, I reacted in a similarly uncomfortable fashion. One weekend, the husbands in our marriage group got together and surprised us wives with a getaway. We all spent a weekend at the beach and had a great time playing, eating, and having Bible studies together.

One evening, after a special dinner the men had planned, they had us all sit in chairs in a circle, and they each brought out a small tub of water.

In turn, each husband knelt down, read something lovely that he had written about his wife, and then proceeded to wash her feet. The moment was beautiful and moving. I was in awe. But at the same time, I was dreading my turn. I squirm under any kind of attention (opening presents in front of people is pretty much a nightmare). But there was another reason for my discomfort.

I struggle even now to define what I was feeling, but it basically boiled down to feeling unworthy. I didn't want my husband kneeling down and washing my feet. It's not like we had never exchanged foot rubs, but this was different. It was humbling. It was uncomfortable. I didn't want him serving me in that way. If anything, I felt I should be washing *his* feet. After all, I am his helpmate. And, let's not forget, everyone was watching. Squirm, squirm, squirm.

About halfway through the foot washing, I began to cry. Watching my strong husband, kneeling, head down, gently washing my feet, while knowing that he was also uncomfortable with everyone's eyes on him, my heart filled with so much gratitude that it spilled right out and washed away my discomfort.

Of all the ways he could have chosen to tell me he loved me, he chose this.

Of all the ways Jesus could have chosen to show His disciples the full extent of His love, He chose this. Knowing He was about to die for them, He chose to serve them in the most humbling way. He chose to literally cleanse them, showing His future followers that He would cleanse their ugliest parts as well.

Next, He encouraged and instructed them, strengthening them for what was to come, and finally, He prayed for them.

Then, He was arrested.

What would you do if you knew you had one last night to show your husband the full extent of your love?

Would you do as Jesus did? Love him in words, action, and prayer? Or would your focus be on yourself, your needs, your wants? Only by the grace of God could I even hope to remember to have Jesus' servant heart at a time like that, let alone act on it.

Author Elizabeth George writes that each day is its own little life, and that how you live each day determines how you live your whole life.[2]

Today, let's live so that we will be content when we look back and see how we have lived. Let's choose to show the full extent of our love.

Reflect

Answer these questions after doing Challenge 1.

How did your husband react to the foot washing?

_____

_____

_____

How did it feel to serve him in this way?

_____

_____

If you completed a challenge today, list it here:

_____

_____

_____

Day Three — A Suitable Helper

Today, I was served by _____ *in this way:* _____

Pray

Pray that you will be the kind of helper your husband needs. Pray that God will help you have a cheerful spirit as you're helping your husband, and that God will show you the ways in which you can best serve him.[3]

Meditate

Read this week's verse twice out loud, then attempt to say it without looking.

Dwell

I am the go-to person if someone needs help with

_____

_____

_____

Breathe

> The LORD God said, "It is not good for the man to be alone. I will make a helper suitable for him."
>
> Genesis 2:18

Too often, wives don't like to be defined as their husband's helper. In the last ten years of mentoring and studying marriage with several women, I see two main negative reactions to this idea. First, some wives bristle when referred to as *helper* because they feel like they've been demoted to a lowly role.

The other reaction I see is women accepting the role, but tragically misunderstanding it. If you believe that your only ministry is to support your husband's ministry, and that your only purpose in life is to help your husband, you may fall into this camp. While those are great aspects of our lives as wives, there is so much we miss out on when we feel we are reduced to just that.

The word *helper* in Genesis 2:18, coming from the Hebrew word *ezer*, is the same word used by David (whom God called a man after His own heart) to describe God as our help in Psalm 115:9–11:

> All you Israelites, trust in the LORD—
> he is their help and shield.
> House of Aaron, trust in the LORD—
> he is their help and shield.
> You who fear him, trust in the LORD—
> he is their help and shield.

Our position as our husband's helper does not lower us in God's estimation. In fact, it elevates our role to one of heavenly importance!

Notice in Genesis, on the sixth day, God doesn't say, "It is not good for man to be so busy. I will create a helper for him." No, He says it's "not good for the man to be alone. I will make a helper suitable for him."

Adam didn't need an assistant—he needed a partner.

Let's look at the difference between the two.

Say the owner of a fairly large company finds himself in need of a little help, so he hires an assistant.

The assistant works for her boss, and her only role in the boss's life is to serve the boss. While a great boss will acknowledge that an assistant is her own person and maybe even ask how she's doing once in a while, it is a mutually agreed upon fact that said assistant's sole purpose in the relationship is to serve. An assistant is the employee; the boss is the employer. An assistant isn't risking much; if the company folds, she goes and gets a new job.

Now let's imagine that the owner of our fictional company is in a little over his head, so he decides to take on a full partner. This is no boss and employee relationship. Partners are equal. They have equal input, equal risk, and equal compensation. The partners come alongside one another and support each other. Sure, the partner may find herself doing some tasks that could be delegated to an assistant, but she's doing them joyfully, since it's her company, too.

Like Adam, your husband doesn't need an assistant. He needs a partner.

Please don't bristle when you hear the word helper, and don't sell yourself short, either. God intended you to be a full partner in your marriage, not an assistant. And when we help our husbands, we're fulfilling part of our purpose in life. It's not our only purpose, but it is a valid and worthy one.

Once you can see yourself properly—as helping your husband in accordance with God's plan, as his loving partner designed just for him—the helping itself doesn't seem so demeaning. It seems right. Righteous, even. And that's good, because it is, and it has been since day one. Or rather, Day Six.

Ten Ways to Be a Suitable Helper, aka a Partner Wife

1. Invest in your marriage. Spend a portion of your time and money on doing things together.
2. Talk about dreams and goals for your family and make plans together for how you can work toward them.

3. Be a good steward of your finances. Agree on a budget and stick to it.

4. Help your husband with the little day-to-day things. Yes, *do* the "assistant" things. (There's a great list on Day Four to help you with this.)

5. Take care of yourself so that you can better contribute to your marriage. Do what you can to stay healthy and strong, and make sure you get plenty of rest and some emotional downtime, too. You'll both be happier for it.

6. Keep studying and learning. As you would with any profession, you can never learn too much about marriage. In addition to the Bible, I like to always be reading some kind of Christian living or spiritual growth book. You're on the right track, participating in this challenge.

7. Work together to intentionally divide the chores in a way that makes sense for your family and keep up with your end of things. Do tasks from his list once in a while, too.

8. Be available for intimacy regularly. See Week One, Day Four for more on this.

9. Be trustworthy and honest. Can his heart safely trust you? (Proverbs 31:11 NLT)

10. Manage your time wisely and make sure you're not allowing idleness to creep in. If you're the one who manages the household calendar and schedule, stay diligent with it and keep the rest of the family in the loop.

Are You a Suitable Helper? A Quiz

For each of the following questions, circle Yes (**Y**) or No (**N**).

Y N 1. Have you prepared a meal for your husband in the last week?

Y N 2. Do you know what your husband's plans are for the next week or so?

Y N 3. Do you usually stick to your budget and not hide any purchases from your husband?

Y N 4. Is your husband fully aware of how you spend your time, and is he in agreement with you about it?

Y N 5. Do you know which household chores are considered yours and do you keep up with them?

Y N 6. Have you helped your husband get prepared for work any day this week? (By packing a lunch, getting his clothes ready, bringing him coffee, etc.)

Y N 7. Have you spent one-on-one time with your husband, just talking at least three times in the last week, even if it's only a few minutes before bed, or on the phone?

Y N 8. Have you been getting plenty of sleep, eating fairly well, and exercising this week?

Y N 9. Have you discussed any problems together this week?

Y N 10. Have you made yourself available for sex in the last week?

Scoring: Give yourself one point for each YES answer.

7–10: You are a Rock Star Helper! You go above and beyond in your role as a wife. Your husband is blessed to have you as a partner. Keep up the good work!

4–6: You are a Suitable Helper! You go out of your way to help your husband and to be there for him. Good work!

2–3: You're giving a good effort, and that might be all you can accomplish with your lifestyle right now. If you feel you could be doing more to help your husband, you'll get lots of ideas with tomorrow's reading.

0–1: Uh-oh. Looks like you haven't been able to help your husband much lately. Why do you think that is? If you've been busy and overwhelmed, cut yourself some slack. Try to add one more helpful thing in the following week, then one more the next, and so on. You'll be a Rock Star Helper in no time.

Reflect

In which of the ten ways to be a suitable helper are you strongest?

_____

_____

In which could you most improve?

_____

_____

If you completed a challenge today, list it here:

_____

Make His Day Easier — Day Four

Today, I was served by _____
in this way: _____

Pray

Pray that your husband will lovingly serve his family, following Christ's own example. Pray that God will strengthen you as you work to serve your husband, and that you will remain humble and obedient to God's Word.[4]

Meditate

Copy this week's memory verse here:

_____

Dwell

My husband's favorite breakfast is

Breathe

One of the simplest ways to serve your husband is to make his day easier. We've already worked on some heart attitudes that might keep us from wanting to help our husbands. Now let's do some practical things to help him and make him feel loved and cared for.

I don't know about you, but sometimes I'll wake up, read my Bible, and have great intentions for helping my husband throughout the day. But then the day gets going, and sometimes the little things I could do for him get put on the back burner as I just focus on getting through the day. I tend to be forgetful more than unwilling.

Here are a few reminders that help me remember to do those little things.

Attach something to a task you already do. If you want to make a habit of bringing your husband coffee in the morning, do it when you pour yourself a cup. Or, every night when you're getting dressed for bed, go over any plans for the next day. Adding something to an existing routine means you have a better chance of making it a habit.

Leave yourself a note. Visual reminders are very helpful.

Set an alarm on your phone. This is a jolting way to be reminded, but it works.

Here are some ideas for ways you can help your husband in every part of the day. See this list as a menu of several choices and opportunities to help your husband. Don't think that anyone can or necessarily *should* do everything on this list. I mean, our guys aren't helpless, and we sure don't want to treat them as if they are. Browse this list with that in mind.

Make His Day Easier List

In the Morning

Prepare his breakfast.

Warm his towel while he's in the shower.

Help him gather what he needs for work.

Pack a lunch for him.

Remind him of any plans for the day.

Make his coffee or a smoothie and bring it to him as he's getting ready, or to have on the way to work.

Send him off with a healthy snack.

In the Afternoon

Run an errand for him.

Make sure he has a place to drop his things when he gets home. (More about this in Bonus Week One.)

Make phone calls for him.

Make sure his laundry is done and he has clean clothes.

Tidy up the bedroom so he has a peaceful place to come home to.

In the Evening

Have dinner ready when he gets home from work.

Do one of his chores.

Take care of something he's been putting off doing.

Take care of something you've been asking him to do, and let him know that you found some time to get it done on your own.

Lay his clothes out for him for the next day.

Run a warm bath for him to soak in if he's had a hard day.

Ask him what you could do to help him tomorrow.

Remind him of any plans for the next day.

Reflect

What things on this list could you do today?

_____

_____

_____

_____

How do you feel about helping your husband?

_____

_____

_____

_____

If you completed a challenge today, list it here: _____

Day Five # When You Need Help

Today, I was served by _____
in this way: _____

Pray

Pray that you will be able to openly communicate with your husband and that you'll speak the truth in love. Pray that God will meet all of your needs according to His riches in Christ Jesus.[5]

Meditate

Write this week's memory verse from memory:

_____

_____

_____

_____

Dwell

My husband is blessed to have a _____ wife.

Breathe

We've read a lot this week about helping and serving our husbands. And I make it pretty clear that I'm writing this book for wives, not husbands. But if you feel continually stressed because you're not getting the help you need, it can make it extra hard to lovingly help your husband.

So while I firmly believe that our focus needs to be on changing ourselves and our hearts, I can't ignore the fact that some of us truly need help getting through to our husbands and letting them know what *we* need from them.

And it's okay to do that.

If you don't address these issues, you run the risk of constantly fighting, keeping it all in until you explode, or letting resentment and bitterness build until that's all that's left.

Learning how to deal with these things and get your needs addressed does actually bless your husband in the long run. You'll have a happier home and a healthier partnership.

What's not to love about that?

Practical Ways to Let Him Know What You Need from Him

First, Pray

Please, don't ever bring up anything big with your husband without praying about it first—even if you just utter a quick prayer and ask God to guide your conversation as you walk toward him. Better yet, tell your husband you'd like to talk about something and pray *with* him first.

Take Stock

Make a list, even a mental one, of everything you feel you need help or support with. Now, pick only one thing to bring up. Take your time and be patient. (That's a breeze, right? Ha.) Once you feel you're working well together on a certain area, try adding another request. This isn't because our husbands are dumb or incapable. We're just being considerate wives as we make adjustments to our lives that maybe no one else was planning on making. It's not kind or fair to dump on him a list of twelve things he needs to start doing differently, stat.

Lead with What You Need

Start by stating what you need and how you feel. "I am busy with work and taking the kids to soccer practice and I could really use your help with dinner."

Or, "I feel hurt when you ignore me when I'm talking. I need you to start paying attention when I speak." The key is to start out by saying, "I . . ."

Avoid placing the blame and saying, "You always . . ." or "You never . . ." Starting with your needs puts him at ease and encourages him to see how he can help you, instead of putting him on the defensive. Look at it as solving a problem together, not as blaming and accusing. It's a kinder way to communicate.

Be Balanced and Fair

If you're asking your husband to work on one thing, it's only fair that you're willing to do the same. Let him know what you need and ask if there's anything you can work on for him. Then be prepared to do it.

Remind without Nagging

Once you've agreed to change a situation, he might need reminders. Yet so often reminders turn to nagging, which turns into resentment or arguments. Then we're right back where we started.

If you're working on behavioral or character changes, it's best to trust God to remind him. We are not our husband's Holy Spirit. When you're making practical changes and you need to make sure something is done, a positive reminder is the way to go.

In the past, if I'd asked my husband to pick up our daughter from a rehearsal after work, I'd send him a text reminder about the time he's getting off work. *Don't forget Sophie!* He would usually reply, *I didn't.* I think he was a little annoyed that I didn't trust him to remember.

But my Mommy heart can't help but remember that one time he did forget a commitment. (Not that he ever forgot a kid, just to be clear.) So these days, I'll text something like, *Thanks again for getting Sophie today!* He probably knows what I'm doing, but it's framed more kindly and no one has to feel nagged.

A good rule of thumb is that if you remind him more than twice, it's probably becoming a nagging situation. We don't want to become like the quarrelsome wife mentioned in Proverbs, so resist the urge to remind over and over again.

A quarrelsome wife is like the dripping of a leaky roof in a rainstorm.

Proverbs 27:15

When He Won't Help

This is a tough one. If you're asking your husband for his help, and he refuses, or if he says he'll help, then doesn't, what is a wife to do? Here are some tips when you find yourself in this situation.

1. Find a Christian couple or a woman you trust and see if a fresh perspective will help. Remember, we don't want to complain about our husbands to others, so make sure you're truly seeking guidance and advice. If you and your husband just flat out disagree, an older couple can talk you through it and share their wisdom with you. If your husband is unwilling, reach out to a godly woman on your own and see if she has any advice for you.

2. If it's a practical issue, find another solution that doesn't involve him. If you've asked him to take care of dinner once a week and he won't or can't do it, order takeout. If you need him to help with rides after school and he won't or can't, enlist the help of a friend. If he has a bad attitude about the whole thing, that can make finding an alternate solution extra aggravating for you. But what else are you going to do? Are you going to keep nagging him and become bitter that he won't help? Or are you going to fix it yourself and move on? The key here is moving on and not storing up resentment because you had to do it yourself.

3. If it's a heart issue, let go and trust God. If you've asked him to be more attentive or less critical, and he won't, take it up in prayer. Keep praying and focusing on the good, thanking

God for all of the praiseworthy things in your life. God does promise us His peace when we do that (Philippians 4:6–7). I can't promise that it's always easy to do, but I can promise that it's worth it. Oftentimes, God will change your husband's heart over time. But sometimes people don't change. You need to find a way to live with his shortcomings and remain a positive wife, and trusting in God is the only way to do that.

Reflect

When upset, are you more likely to hold things in until you explode, or argue constantly?

_____

What do you think your husband would ask you to work on?

_____

_____

If you completed a challenge today, list it here:

_____

Weekend Reflection

What did the term *helper* as used in Genesis 2:18 make you think of before reading Day Three's Breathe section?

_____

_____

_____

_____

What do you think of it now?

_____

_____

_____

What did you choose from the Make His Day Easier List?

_____

_____

_____

_____

How has God used your weaknesses to strengthen you?

_____

_____

What is your favorite way to serve your husband?

_____

_____

_____

Weekly Goal Check-In

How did you do with noticing how you were served this week?

_____

Did it change your outlook at all?

_____

_____

How do you think being aware of this will help you as you go forward?

_____

_____

_____

Mid-Challenge Check-In

Below is a post I shared in our *Bless Your Husband* Daily Facebook Group. It really resonated with the wives there, and I think it might with you, too. As we head into Week Three, I wanted to set some time aside to encourage you before you jump in.

You are awesome. Even if you skip a ton of challenges. Even if you sort of feel like a crummy wife sometimes. God sees your heart and He knows your desire is to love and bless your husband.

Sure, sometimes you fall short, but hey, you're trying. And that, my friend, is what matters. A lot. Don't let the enemy convince you that trying is worthless, and definitely don't let him convince you that you're worthless.

I know some of you are struggling in your marriage. Maybe your husband is ungrateful and maybe he's even kind of a jerk. And maybe you find yourself wondering why you even bother doing this.

Just remember, we're not doing this to earn anyone's favor. Not your husband's and not God's. Things like this change us and when good change starts happening, the enemy does not like it. And maybe you don't see any changes yet. But know that the enemy doesn't attack someone who is not a threat.

So don't forget to cover yourself in prayer as you go about the challenge of being a godly wife. Don't forget to spend time in God's Word. Reach out to a friend if you need to.

Stay the course!
And lastly, let's all remember this:

Whatever you do, work at it with all your heart, as working for the Lord, not for human masters, since you know that you will receive an inheritance from the Lord as a reward. It is the Lord Christ you are serving.

Colossians 3:23–24

The Barnabas Wife

How sweet are your words to my taste,
sweeter than honey to my mouth!

Psalm 119:103

Joseph, a Levite from Cyprus, was the apostle Paul's companion on his missionary trips. He was given the nickname Barnabas, "which means 'son of encouragement'" (Acts 4:36).

Can you imagine if our nicknames today were based on character traits?

Nicknames are often formed based on physical traits. One of my grandmas was nicknamed Grandma Pudgy by her family. I'm not sure why, since she was thin for as long as I knew her. Big men are sometimes called Tiny, and redheads are sometimes called Red.

Nicknames based on character traits are far less common, though I suppose we all know of a Debbie Downer or a Nervous Nellie. However, I doubt they actually got stuck with that as their given name, and they certainly didn't go down in the history of the world's greatest Book being called that.

Yet Barnabas's nickname was recorded in Scripture. Like, forever! This makes me wonder just how encouraging he was. He must have had encouraging words spilling out of him in every circumstance to have earned that name.

My family calls me Ang, and the friends who know me best, or who have known me the longest and gotten close to my family tend to call me by that name.

I wonder what my nickname would be if it was based on my character as a wife? Perhaps sometimes it would be Daughter of Kindness, though I suspect more often it would be Child of Impatience. I'd like to think it could be Mother of Wisdom, following in the footsteps of the beautiful Proverbs 31 woman, but I think I've got *at least* a few more years before I can reach that status.

What would your wifely nickname be? Did you shudder a little to think of it? Let's not be too hard on ourselves. My guess is that we all have at least two or three character traits that bless the socks off our husbands. And we probably have one or two he could live without.

Let's focus on feeding and growing the good stuff inside of us.

This week, we're going to be Barnabas Wives. We're going to encourage our husbands in different areas, and we're going to speak words that are so soothing and healing, we might as well be called Barnabas.

But first, we must fill our own cups so we can overspill and bless others.

Day One   Filled to Overflowing

We're going to start by studying who and what God says we are. In doing so, you will realize just how fully loved you are by your

Creator, and when your cup is filled with that knowledge, it will overflow and bless others.

You'll be a Barnabas Wife before you know it.

You are:

God's child. "Yet to all who did receive him, to those who believed in his name, he gave the right to become children of God" (John 1:12).

Accepted. "Accept one another, then, just as Christ accepted you, in order to bring praise to God" (Romans 15:7).

Made in God's image. "So God created mankind in his own image, in the image of God he created them; male and female he created them" (Genesis 1:27).

Cherished. "Can a mother forget the baby at her breast and have no compassion on the child she has borne? Though she may forget, I will not forget you!" (Isaiah 49:15)

Redeemed. "For you know that it was not with perishable things such as silver or gold that you were redeemed from the empty way of life handed down to you from your ancestors, but with the precious blood of Christ, a lamb without blemish or defect" (1 Peter 1:18–19).

Capable. "I can do all things through Christ who gives me strength" (Philippians 4:13).

Wonderfully made. "I praise you because I am fearfully and wonderfully made; your works are wonderful, I know that full well" (Psalm 139:14).

Planned. "Your eyes saw my unformed body; all the days ordained for me were written in your book before one of them came to be" (Psalm 139:16).

Loved. "The Lord appeared to us in the past, saying: 'I have loved you with an everlasting love; I have drawn you with unfailing kindness'" (Jeremiah 31:3).

Weekly Goal

We can't become expert encouragers if we ourselves are empty. We all have traits, whether physical or emotional, that we wish we didn't have, but the list above shows who God says we are.

Instead of dwelling on what you don't like, think on what God says about you this week, and decide to love the way He made you. Each day, you'll fill in the statement below to reinforce this idea and help you grow in acceptance of who you are as God's child.

Choose a phrase from the list above that you struggle to believe and fill in the blank below.

This week, I will believe in my heart and mind that I am

_____

_____

Memory Verse

> Gracious words are a honeycomb,
> sweet to the soul and healing to the bones.
> Proverbs 16:24

Write this week's memory verse on a sticky note or index card and post it on your bathroom mirror or somewhere you'll see it often.

Week Three Challenges

1. Send your husband a photo of the two of you together at a happy time, and add a note telling him how much you love your happy memories. If you don't have smartphones, get a print and put it on his nightstand or dresser with a little note. #byhhappytimes

2. Reminisce with your husband about when you met, your first date, your first kiss, or some other happy time. Just strike up a conversation and start with "Remember when . . ." My kids have always liked hearing these stories, too, so you don't necessarily need to be alone to do this. (Though they might judge you when they're older if you let it slip that you kissed on the first date. Don't ask me how I know this.) #byhmemories

3. Write out an encouraging Scripture and put it somewhere your husband will find it during the day. Put a sticky note on his steering wheel, in his briefcase, in his wallet, or in his packed lunch. #byhscripture

4. Write a nice post about your husband on social media today. If you're not on social media, you can praise him in front of others for the same effect. #byhlovemyhusband

5. Encourage your husband, in a tangible way, to spend time with his friends. Get him a certificate for a round of golf, a gift card to his favorite sports bar, concert tickets, or something else that he can do with a friend. Determine to be cheerful when he leaves and when he comes back. Bacon is optional. #byhfriendtime

6. If you haven't done it yet, print out one of the notecards available on my website and fill it out for your husband. (Instructions for accessing online content are on page 196.) #byhblessyourhusbandcards

7. Put a reminder on your phone every day this week, or a sticky note on your Bible that says, "Be a Barnabas Wife." #byhbarnabaswife

Day Two Married, Social Media Style

(This week for your goal, simply write your statement of God's truth about yourself every day in the space provided. Say it out loud and believe it!)

God says that I am _____,
and He doesn't lie!

Pray

Pray that God would give you insight on how to best encourage your husband. Pray that when the time comes, He will give you authentic words that He knows will bless your husband.[1]

Meditate

As you look at your memory verse today, highlight or underline the verse in your Bible. Put a heart next to the verse, so you'll remember to love your husband this way.

Dwell

My husband encourages me to

_____

Breathe

A couple of years ago, I started getting fed up with social media and I was considering deleting all of my accounts. I was tired of all of the negativity, and it seemed that every time I logged on, there was some new drama or ugly debate among friends there. I was getting upset to the point where I couldn't ignore it, so the obvious solution was to stay off of social media for a while.

So I did. I didn't deactivate my accounts, but I deleted all the apps from my phone so they weren't as easily accessible and stayed away for a couple of weeks. During that time, I had to admit that I was feeling better emotionally. But I also missed the pleasant side of social media. I missed feeling connected to friends and family I hardly ever get to see, and I missed some of the uplifting groups I belonged to.

So, I went back, but I decided to do a sort of encouragement experiment on Facebook. Every day, I would tag someone and write what I loved about that person. It wasn't long before getting on Facebook was an entirely new and improved experience. I was greeted by warm messages, loving comments, and best of all, my friends and family were feeling loved and encouraged. Some of my friends even followed suit and began posting their own encouraging messages for their family and friends.

Like all good things, my experiment came to an end. But the effects lingered. I had a better attitude toward Facebook, asking myself what good I could bring every day, and it became easier to just scroll past things that were going to cause me stress or to dwell on ugliness.

Even to this day, those posts I did for those months still pop up in my Facebook "memories" every once in a while, and I am reminded that it's good to tell people that you love them and why.

A few years ago, we faced a death in our family. At the time, several of my Facebook friends posted on my wall and left encouraging, thoughtful messages and comments. I didn't notice all of them at the time, because it was such a strained time for us. But again, a year later, these posts started coming up in my "memories" on Facebook.

The kind words soothed my spirit all over again, and I was touched as I read some posts that I had missed the first time around. A whole year later on the anniversary of this death, these posts lifted my spirits and it gave me peace to know that we had so many loved ones praying for us.

You never know how your words may impact someone, and what ripple effect that may have in their life. In these days when social media can turn ugly very quickly, why not be a voice that shines a light in the darkness? Ask yourself how you can use social media for good, and do so.

I know you won't be surprised when I say, let's start with our husbands.

Publicly Thank Him

When you start to focus on the good, you begin to notice more and more positive things. Thank your husband for some of the nice things he does for you and the family. Once in awhile, take your thanks to social media and let the world know you're thankful for him.

Share His Successes

Did your husband get a promotion recently? Did he spend a weekend working hard on your backyard? Let him know you're proud of him by posting photos and saying what a good job he did.

Encourage Him

Without sharing anything too personal, you can ask your friends to pray for him and to leave an encouraging word if he's sick or going through a rough time. Respect his privacy at all costs, but if he could use some encouragement, don't be afraid to ask others for it.

Hide an inside joke in your post to him. If I posted, "Looking forward to our date tonight! I'll bring the apples!" Only my husband would know what I meant and it would give him a smile meant just for him.

Flirt with Him

Leave heart eyes on his photos, or comments saying how cute he is. Post happy photos of the two of you together; make your profile photo a picture of the two of you and add a frame of hearts. Write him the occasional love-note post. Basically, act like a teenage girl with her first boyfriend.

Respect Him

Make sure that your own profile makes it clear you're married. Unless you're using a professional profile for business reasons, your personal profiles should indicate that you're happily married. It might not cut down on messages from random princes of Nigeria, but it may cut down on ex-boyfriends trying to distract you, and it will definitely show your husband he is a priority.

Respect his privacy. Don't overshare about the mysterious rash he has, or that he's been really depressed and crying lately. Just don't.

Consider his personality. My husband is private about some things, but he doesn't mind me being cheesy for all to see. Your guy might not want his boss and co-workers to see your mushy gushy posts, even if they are sweet. Same goes for photos. Only share what he's comfortable with.

Be Considerate

Avoid causing jealousy. While we want to build our men up and appreciate them, we also don't want to cause other wives to stumble with jealousy. Be careful not to overdo it and share how amazing your husband is several times a day. You can do that privately as much as you like.

Make sure, too, that your motivation isn't to make your friends jealous. God is all about our heart's intention, so be sure your only goal is to bless your husband. And be sensitive. If your best friend just found out that her husband is cheating on her, you might want to rethink that post about your husband bringing you breakfast in bed.

Social Media Mad Lib

Fill in the words, then add them in order to the paragraph below. You've just created a fun, mushy post to share about your husband.

1. Nickname you have for your husband _____
2. How long have you been married? _____
3. A verb your husband does well _____
4. Adjective to describe your life _____
5. Adjective to describe your husband _____
6. His name _____
7. Another word for love _____

I'm feeling extra thankful for my _____ today. I can't believe we've been married _____ years. Time flies when you're having fun! I love how he _____ and I can't imagine our _____ life without him. Thanks for being a _____ husband, _____. I _____ you!

Reflect

How does social media affect your marriage, if at all?

_____

_____

Have you ever "fasted" from social media? What did you learn?

_____

_____

_____

If you completed a challenge today, list it here:

_____

_____

_____

Purposeful Reminiscing Day Three

God says that I am _____,
and He doesn't lie!

Pray

Pray for your husband's mind to be set apart for God, and that he will be able to keep his mind on heavenly things. Pray that he'll be able to renew his mind and that his thoughts would be pleasing to God.[2]

Meditate

Read this week's verse twice out loud, then attempt to say it without looking.

Dwell

The first place my husband and I lived was

_____

_____

_____

Breathe

My mom is an amazing storyteller. Throughout my childhood, she regaled us with richly woven dramatic tales of her life. To this day, I can recall certain stories she told us, and tears come to my eyes as the same feelings I had the first time I heard the story wash over me. We heard fun stories of her childhood in the fifties and sixties, and crazy accounts of growing up with three sisters in one small bedroom. We learned about her early days of marriage and her life as a young mom in the seventies. Sure, we heard many of the stories repeated again and again, but we didn't mind. In fact, we craved them. We were so familiar with them that it was like a part of her past belonged to us, too.

Once I had kids of my own, the storytelling continued. My girls can tell you all about what it was like for me to grow up with three brothers and about my school days in the nineties.

My daughter was visiting a friend once and asked her friend's mom what her childhood was like. She was shocked when she said the mom had never told her children one thing about her upbringing, nonchalantly saying, "They never asked." She was happy to share a couple of stories with my daughter, while the friend rolled her eyes and said, "This is boring."

"Mom," my daughter came home and told me that night, "can you even imagine? How do you live that long and not know about your mom's life?" She was the ripe old age of thirteen at the time, but I understood what she meant.

I couldn't imagine. I'd been brought up by a great storyteller, and I guess I figured all families were that way. And you know what? I think all families should be that way.

In Week One, we spent some time looking back, remembering the wife we were when we were first married. Today, we're going to look back again and do something I like to call *purposeful reminiscing*.

Naturally, we're going to apply this to our marriage. Thinking about happy times you've had with your husband tends to bring up pleasant, warm feelings. And who doesn't love those?

When we go a step further and reminisce with our husbands, we're passing those pleasant feelings on to him. We're reminding him that we are a couple and *we* share a past, and that we have lots more fun to look forward to. When you're reminiscing together, he may remember bits that you don't, and vice versa. Your memories become fuller and more real with two points of view. And it just feels good.

You don't have to be an incredible storyteller like my mom to keep your memories alive. A simple "Remember when . . ." is enough to get those good feelings flowing. Read on for some reminiscing tips.

Find an Anchor

A diet program I followed once suggested the idea of having an anchor. An anchor was an object you looked at that reminded you of something you had been successful at before. The idea was to remind yourself of past success and that you could succeed again with weight loss. I chose my wedding ring for my anchor. At the time, I had lost enough of the baby weight that my ring fit again, after not being able to wear it while I was pregnant. I still had a ways to go, but at least I'd lost enough for my ring to fit.

The problem was, every time I looked at my ring and tried to remind myself of being successful with weight loss, my mind just pictured the day my husband proposed to me. I remembered him putting the ring on my finger, and how his face looked when he said, "Will you marry me?"

It wasn't exactly helping with the diet, but it had an unexpected, pleasant effect.

Quite a few years later, after surgeries and health issues, I'd gained some weight again, and I wasn't the tiny little bride I had been when my husband proposed to me. My ring didn't fit anymore. I hadn't wanted to have it resized because I felt I would be admitting I would never be at my wedding weight again. It took a few years, but I finally realized that I needed that anchor. My ring means too much to me to let it sit in a drawer. It belongs on my finger, where I can see it and be reminded of why I said *I do*. So I finally had it resized so I could wear it again.

Can you find an anchor of your own? Something to look at that will cause you to remember how far you've come as a couple, successes you've had, and how you're meant to be together?

Of course, we don't need a material object to be able to reminisce. Our memories are free for the taking, anytime we choose, but an anchor can be a pleasant reminder.

Preserve Your Memories

Unless your husband is a photographer or scrapbooking enthusiast, the task of keeping memories will probably fall on your shoulders. You don't need to be a crafter and create glorious albums to do this. It can be as simple as taking photos and storing them digitally or in photo albums. Or, jot a few lines down in a journal.

I love taking photos, and with smartphones, it's such an easy way to keep memories. Years from now, you'll look back on your happy times and have lots of opportunities to reminisce. It's also nice for your family to have a little bit of your legacy preserved for them.

Avoid the Two Deadly Cs

Be careful not to compare and complain. When I think back on our dating days, I could easily get annoyed that my husband is no longer wooing me like he did back then. I could compare our relationship now, which is stronger and much more fulfilling, but only see the negatives. We're not as spontaneous; we don't go out as often. We'll talk more about comparison and complaining later, but for now, be aware and don't fall into that trap.

Reminisce Wisely

We can choose what to think back on. Sure, I can remember fights and bad choices and ruined moments. But why would I waste my time doing that? Yes, we should learn from our mistakes, but we shouldn't dwell on them.

Why not fill my heart with happy memories instead, and build upon those?

Reflect

What is the happiest memory you have with your husband?

_____

_____

_____

_____

_____

Is there an anchor you can use to keep your mind focused on good things? Write about what your anchor means to you.

_____

_____

_____

_____

_____

If you completed a challenge today, list it here:

_____

_____

_____

Day Four
Encouraging Him with Scripture

God says that I am _____,
and He doesn't lie!

Pray

Pray that your husband will have a deep desire to study the Word of God. Pray that the Bible will be living and active in his life, and that he would meditate on God's law, day and night.[3]

Meditate

Copy this week's memory verse here:

_____
_____
_____
_____
_____

Dwell

My favorite Proverb is _____
_____
_____
_____
_____

Breathe

All Scripture is God-breathed and is useful for teaching, rebuking, correcting and training in righteousness, so that the servant of God may be thoroughly equipped for every good work.

2 Timothy 3:16–17

Before exploring some practical ways to encourage your husband with God's Word, let's look at the many reasons we should incorporate Scripture into our marriage.

Lift your husband when he's down. Your husband is so loved by the God who created him. Find verses to lift his spirits when he's feeling sad or down.

Point him to an awesome God. When life is overwhelming, we all need to be reminded that God is in control. Our husbands are no different. Encourage yours with Scripture that reminds him of who God is and how much He loves and cares for us.

Encourage the strengths you see in him. There is no better way to encourage your husband than with the truth of God's Word. On Day One of this week, you read a list of what and who God says you are. This list applies to your husband as well, and is a good place to start encouraging him.

Advise him. If your husband asks for your opinion or advice, it's helpful to already be knowledgeable about God's Word so you can share sound, biblical wisdom.

Encourage him to stay strong in the Lord. The Bible should be read over and over again. Every day, we need to be reminded of God's love, God's power, and God's commands. Encourage your husband to stay strong in following Jesus by speaking Scripture into his life. And if your husband is a *super believer*? If he's so much wiser than you and farther along in his walk with God? Rest assured, he still needs his godly wife to encourage him in the Lord. And take heart that God uses the weak to help the strong!

If your husband is not a believer, *witness to him without saying a word*. Pay special attention to modeling Scripture in your own life. If he seems open to your sending him verses, then by all means, do so. If it aggravates him and causes arguments, remember what Peter said:

> Wives, in the same way submit yourselves to your own husbands so that, if any of them do not believe the word, they may be won over without words by the behavior of their wives, when they see the purity and reverence of your lives.
>
> 1 Peter 3:1–2

You can still pray Scripture over him without involving him. You can speak God's truths without quoting the Scriptures and aggravating him. God's Word never returns void. You can give him wise advice based on what you know God would want. How blessed is the man who has a godly wife!

If you don't know where to find all this Scripture to encourage him, try searching a topical concordance or use a website like Bible Gateway. When you're doing your own Bible study, or listening to sermons or podcasts, make a note when you hear something that may be useful to your husband.

Cautions

Avoid scolding your husband via Scripture. Not that any of us would do *that*, right? But be careful that you're using God's Word correctly, and not trying to scold or shame your husband. I suggest leaving those things for your prayer life, and unless your husband asks for advice, steer clear of trying to rebuke him with Scripture. If you feel led to confront him on a serious topic, armed with Scripture, be sure you've prayed first and have a gentle spirit.

Focus on the good. Don't judge yourself harshly or feel like you're failing if you go a few days and forget to mention Scripture to your husband. You're sprinkling something positive over your lives, not adding something else to be checked off your daily to-do list.

Speaking to one another with psalms, hymns, and songs from the
Spirit. Sing and make music from your heart to the Lord.

Ephesians 5:19

Practical Ways to Encourage Him in the Word

There are many quick and easy ways to encourage your husband
in the Word, such as writing a Scripture verse on a note and leaving it for him to find, or texting him a Bible verse. Here are just
a few more.

Speak God's Word Out Loud

There is something about God's Word being spoken that
changes things. I'll often read a verse aloud as I come across it,
even if I am the only one home. When we're all together as a
family, I'll often share a verse that encouraged me or convicted
me that day.

Send Encouraging Memes

Memes are shareable digital photos with words printed on
them. You can find these on Pinterest, or in a Bible app. There's
nothing wrong with sending flowery, feminine memes, but there
are some out there that have manly backgrounds that he might
like, and therefore be more likely to use as his phone's wallpaper
or even send on to a friend.

Use Scripture in Your Own Life

He's probably already seeing your memory verses on the bathroom mirror. Be conscious of sharing your own insights after
Bible study, or referring to a Scripture when explaining to him a
decision you've made. If your husband is already rooted deeply
in Scripture, he'll be blessed to see his wife growing as well. If he

has some growing to do in this area, you're setting a wonderful example without preaching to him.

Find a Verse to Pray over Him

Every year on January 1, I pick a verse to pray over each of my family members. First, I pray and ask God to tug on my heart when I come across the right verse for each person. Then, I'll pray that verse over them all year. I don't actually do this out loud, but during my own quiet prayer time. Sometimes, I'll also pray out loud over my husband, and Scripture comes pouring out of my heart as we're praying. The more Scripture we have stored up in us, the more we can pour out over our husbands.

If you need ideas on how to get started doing this, most of the prayers you'll read in this book are based on Scripture, with the specific references provided in the Notes section.

Your husband is going to be so blessed having a wife who encourages him in the Word. You can't possibly know the effect it could have on his day and on his heart.

Reflect

Use a website search to find an encouraging Bible verse for each of the following situations. List the addresses below, so you'll be ready to use them for yourself and your husband when the need arises. Simply search "Bible verses for when . . ." and plenty of options should come up.

When you're sad _____

When you're tired_____

When you're feeling worthless_____

When you've made a mistake_____

When you're angry_____

When you need wisdom_____

If you completed a challenge today, list it here: _____

Encouraging Man-Friend Time Day Five

God says that I am _____,
and He doesn't lie!

Pray

Pray for your husband's friendships to be blessed. Pray over his close friends, and pray that your husband would do unto others as he would have others do unto him. Pray for his friends to be of good character and that their conversations would be full of grace.[4]

Meditate

Write this week's memory verse from memory:

_____

_____

_____

Dwell

I excel at encouraging my husband in

_____

Breathe

Watch any American sitcom and it won't be long before you hear the wife complaining about her husband's guy time. Even back in the fifties, Lucy and Ethel were constantly trying to crash *boys' night*. Fast-forward to the new millennium and not much has changed. Just the other night, I watched a new show, and they were in the same old situation, with the wife complaining about the husband going to play golf with his buddies. It's interesting just how little the dynamics of marriage as played out on television have changed. While it wasn't as hilarious as Lucy's antics, the core attitude was the same: *Why should he get to go out and have fun, while I'm stuck at home?*

What if we became wives who not only didn't complain about our husbands spending time with their friends, but actually encouraged it?

Now, don't get me wrong. I don't think men should spend more time with their friends than they do with their family, and I don't think women should be stuck at home all of the time, either. But I think many of us could do a whole lot less complaining and find a better way to think about man-friend time.

> As iron sharpens iron, so one person sharpens another.
>
> Proverbs 27:17

When your husband is able to spend time with his friends, he's nurturing a different part of himself. He'll be happier and healthier, which will benefit the whole family. Hopefully, at least some of his friends are godly men. He can be encouraged in his relationship with God during this time, and also encourage others.

Of course, not every guy wants man-friend time, and we have to respect that, too. Though iron sharpens iron, and we hope God will lead each of us into fellowship, there may be seasons in your man's life when he doesn't want that. At all. As an introvert, I understand this completely. We're not all wired to want a group of people around us all of the time.

Once, I decided to encourage my husband in his man time and got him a poker set. He enjoyed playing cards, and I thought it would be fun for him to have a game night. So I gave him the set and told him I would make all of his favorite snacks for his buddies anytime he wanted to play, and hinted that he might like a weekly game.

Eric thought it was pretty cool. So he joined a group that was already established and gave it a shot.

The next week, he didn't want to go back for some reason or another. And then the next week, same thing. Some excuse. The following week, I asked if he wanted the guys to come to our house and he vehemently said, "No!"

He finally told me that he was disappointed in the group, and that he didn't want to tell me why because I was friends with most of the men and, more important, with their wives. *Ah.* At this point, I figured out that even though this group was made up of Christian men, they weren't acting like it. He then told me in no uncertain terms that he wouldn't be joining the poker group. He said he'd rather be at home enjoying his wife and kids. I have never respected my husband more.

And even though I thought it would be good for him to have some man-friend time, this wasn't the kind of group I should be encouraging him to join.

However, there have been plenty of other opportunities to be accepting of his time with friends. I've learned to encourage these times and to welcome him home happily.

My friend Gary, who used to teach a marriage Bible study we were in, gave me great insight into this idea. Gary is a surfer, and that means getting up early on weekends and beating Los Angeles traffic to make it to the beach before sunrise. The men in our marriage class started joining him on some Saturday mornings, which caused some of the wives to complain.

Gary, like my husband, worked hard all week. And all he wanted was to go relieve some stress on his first day off each week. To be honest, I didn't really care that my husband was going surfing, because I would rather sleep in anyway. But I saw the point of the wives who were upset. And their comments got me thinking. He was out there surfing with cute girls in bikinis, while I was stuck home with two kids! Sometimes, I would make petty comments to Eric when he got home. Mostly, I wanted him to be appreciative of my great and noble sacrifice.

One week at Bible study, in the midst of the complaining, Gary asked, "Wouldn't it be great if we just came home to happy wives and bacon?" All the men nodded in agreement.

Something in me just clicked in that moment. *They don't want much,* I thought. From that moment on, I listened to the rational voice in my head that knew these times were good for my husband, instead of the irrational one that said, "What about me?" I strived to be a positive, happy wife to come home to, and my husband was happier for it. Of course, so was I.

Eric's surfing phase didn't last very long, because everyone got older and life got busy. But I still strive to be the happy wife he comes home to when he's had some time with friends.

That's not to say that my petty side doesn't still rear its head once in a while. But now, I make more of an effort to banish these thoughts and focus on loving my husband in words and actions.

Sometimes, I even cook bacon.

Reflect

As you focus on your husband's friend time, make sure you have time with your friends, as well, to sharpen and refresh you. If you're feeling particularly resentful about your husband's time with friends, maybe it's because you've been neglecting this need of your own. How could you make more time for friends?

How do you think your husband would finish Gary's sentence, if not with bacon? "Wouldn't it be great if we came home to happy wives and _____?" Could you make this happen?

_____

If you completed a challenge today, list it here:

_____

Weekend Reflection

What do you think your wifely nickname would be if it was based on your personality?

_____

How large a role does social media play in your day? What are some pitfalls you've noticed?

_____

_____

_____

Did you use an anchor this week to focus on good things? How did that work for you?

_____

_____

_____

How did you encourage your husband with Scripture this week?

_____

_____

_____

Did you encourage your husband to have time with his friends this week? How did he take it?

_____

_____

_____

Weekly Goal Check-In

How did writing out God's true statement about you and saying it out loud help change your mind this week?

_____

_____

_____

Has this knowledge made it from your head to your heart yet? Why or why not?

_____

_____

_____

How do you think being aware of this will help you as you go forward?

_____

_____

_____

The Beautiful Wife

Charm is deceptive and beauty is fleeting,
   but a woman who fears the Lord is to be praised.

Proverbs 31:30

Yes, we know all too well that beauty is fleeting. Perhaps because I went through so many health issues in my twenties, growing older has never bothered me very much. I try not to obsess over each new wrinkle, and instead be happy that I am still blessed to be alive. But every so often I'll get sidetracked and start focusing on all the ways beauty has, well, run fleeing from my life.

Most often, this happens when I come across an old photo of myself, looking all young and gorgeous. I compare it to what I see in the mirror now and start complaining. Yep, I indulge in the two big Cs that I tell you to avoid. Comparing and complaining suck the life right out of you, don't they? We'll be talking about that this week and next, so for now, let's zero in on real beauty.

I'm not going to act like we don't already understand what true beauty is, that it's what's inside that counts and makes us beautiful.

But knowing these things in our minds, believing them in our hearts, and showing them in our actions are very different things.

If inner beauty counts more than outer beauty, then we must spend more time on beautifying our insides, right? That means I would spend more time praying, reading my Bible, and helping others than I do putting on my makeup and doing my hair every day. And I'd spend more time learning about who Jesus is than I would dwelling on that pesky wrinkle in the middle of my forehead. I'd spend more time serving others than I do trying to reach my perfect weight.

I'm not saying we shouldn't have a beauty routine every day. I am one of those women who still likes to put on makeup and do my hair as often as possible, and I don't see anything wrong with that. It becomes wrong when my thoughts become so focused on superficial things that I don't have time to grow in character or to be the woman God calls me to be.

We all know of beautiful women who are superficial or mean. Do they not realize that their time of being considered beautiful by the world is fleeting? One day their looks will fade and all they'll be left with is the shallow shell of the person they've become. A pretty face can only hide so much.

On the other hand, we all know of beautiful women who grow lovelier with age. Their love of God shines through on their face, making them almost glow with a radiance that no bottled cream can come close to re-creating.

My friend Kathy is one of these women. She's a pastor's wife, a mom to four, a grandmother to seven, a worship leader, a painter, a constant encourager, and a mighty prayer warrior. I don't think I've ever seen her when she hasn't asked me how I'm feeling or how something is coming along and let me know that she's praying for me. She's the sweetest woman you'll ever meet, but she has an awesomely sassy side, too. She is always helping someone or serving somewhere. Kathy has always been a petite blond beauty, and the longer I know her, the prettier and prettier she gets. She honestly glows with the love of Jesus.

Sometimes I look at celebrities who are ten years older than me and offhandedly think, *Wow! I hope I look that good when I'm her age!* But what I truly hope is that I look as good as Kathy does now. I hope I'm as kind as she is, and as creative—and so powerfully in love with the Lord that it literally shines on my face.

So how do we live a life that increases our inner beauty?

Spend More Time with Jesus Than with the Mirror

This is going to sound harsh, but if you're spending more time in front of a mirror on a daily basis than you do with Jesus, you have a problem. I'm not suggesting that we become legalistic about it, but if you're spending two hours each day getting ready, and yet don't have time to read your Bible, it's time to check your priorities. There is no substitute for spending time in prayer and in reading the Bible. There just isn't. Make sure you make time for that in your life, and you'll be a beautiful woman.

Apply God's Word to Your Life

It's not enough to just read the Bible, we have to put God's Word into practice. If you're unsure of how to do this, try getting a guided Bible study book.

Have a Thankful Spirit

Focusing on all you have to be thankful for will chase away the complaints and the comparisons. I like to keep an ongoing list in my prayer notebook of things I am thankful for. It's grown to several pages over time, and it's always good to look back and see all of the amazing things, both big and small, that God has done in my life.

Serve Others More Than Yourself

When our focus is on others, it takes the focus off ourselves. A servant's heart makes any woman beautiful. I am a chronic dieter, and I have to be careful that I don't let whatever diet I'm currently on overwhelm my days. I only have so many hours in a day, and if I waste the majority of them worrying about what I'm going to eat next, or how to combine foods or what to avoid, or how many calories are in this or that, then I don't have much time left to focus on what others need. I may end up nice and slim, but I'll be selfish and disconnected from those around me in the end.

Let's allow our quest for outer beauty and health to motivate us, but not consume us.

Day One — The Beauty of Praise

This week we aim to spend more time on beautifying our insides than we do on our appearance. So choose to spend more time praising God for who He is.

Weekly Goal

Set a goal to praise God for a certain number of minutes each day and strive to meet your goal on at least five days. Don't fret about how many minutes to shoot for. Even one minute of turning your thoughts to praising the Lord will make a difference in your life.

For at least five days this week, I will spend ___ minutes praising God for who He is.

When we praise God by acknowledging who He is, we're not only offering up a sacrifice of praise, we are reminding ourselves of who we serve. God is an awesome God with many praiseworthy attributes. If you don't know how to start, read the Psalms and say them out loud to the Lord.

Another way I love to praise God is through music. There are endless praise songs that you can look up and sing along with. I try to start each day with a song of praise. Once this becomes a habit, you'll find more and more things to praise God for. He is good, worthy, loving, just, merciful, Creator, Everlasting Father, Prince of Peace, all-powerful, all-knowing . . . I could go on *all* day!

A good time to do this would be before or after doing your daily challenge. If this seems like too much to add on to your day, consider cutting a few minutes from your morning routine to make time while we're focusing on inner beauty!

Memory Verse

Charm is deceptive, and beauty is fleeting; but a woman who fears the Lord is to be praised.

Proverbs 31:30

Write this week's memory verse on a sticky note or index card and post it on your bathroom mirror or somewhere you'll see it often.

Week Four Challenges

1. Wear something your husband likes to see you in, wear jewelry he's given you, or do your hair in a style he likes. Don't be shy, you can tell him you wore it for him if you really want him to get the point. In the future, you won't always be so obvious, but a little hint never hurt anyone. #byhdressing forhim

2. Take some time and write out three good traits God gave your husband. You don't have to show him, just keep it to yourself and pull your list out once in a while so you can dwell on the good things. Over time, you may want to add to this list, and one day give it to your husband. But for now, let's start with three things. #byh3things

3. Initiate some extra cuddle time today. Spending time snuggling with your guy will improve your mood and his!

4. Pamper yourself. Take a hot bath, paint your nails or have them done, or buy yourself a new face cream. Don't skip this challenge, because it's for yourself. Rest in knowing that you'll be happy and well rested, and that always makes for a more lovely wife. #byhlovelywifey

5. Go on an after-dinner walk with your husband. Without distractions, hold hands and ask him about his day, or just be quiet and enjoy the peace of the outdoors. (No hashtag for this, since we're supposed to be distraction-free on our walk.)

6. Spend five minutes getting pretty before you see him this evening. Brush your hair, get dressed if you're not already, have a mint. Set a timer and see how much you can do in five minutes. #byhgettingpretty

7. Photo op! Get pretty and take a photo with your husband. If you can't afford a professional photographer, take a selfie or have a friend or one of your kids take it. Frame the photo and display it somewhere in your house. For added fun, add a heart-filled frame on social media and change your profiles to this photo for at least a week. #byhphotoblessing

Dress for Him

Today, I praised God for ___ minutes.

Pray

Pray that you would be a woman who fears the Lord and that your beauty would come from the unfading loveliness of a gentle and quiet spirit, which is of great worth in God's sight.[1]

Meditate

As you look at your memory verse today, highlight or underline the verse in your Bible. Also read Proverbs 31:10–31, which describes the noble wife. Let's pay close attention to those words!

Dwell

An outfit I feel and look great in is _____.

Breathe

So maybe you read the title for today and thought I meant dressing for the Lord. While that would be a great topic, I actually meant dressing for your husband. I know some of you are wincing at the title of today's reading, and I understand. But please bear with me and read on to see how we can maintain our individuality and still bless our husbands in this way.

One time, when Eric and I were dating, he came to pick me up for a night out. He came in and sat down, then said, "Oh, I'll wait for you to change." I blushed and said, "Um, I already did."

I was wearing baggy fabric pants known as palazzo pants and a little sweater vest with a baby tee under it. It wasn't the sexiest look, but it was cute and trendy and I felt good in it. I guess Eric was more accustomed to the skimpy dresses I wore back then. He wrinkled his nose. "Is that what you're wearing?" he asked. I felt we had already established that it was, so I just gave him a dirty look.

"You don't like it?" I said.

"No, it's just that it doesn't really show how . . ." He paused, looking for the right word. "How sexy you are. You don't look as good as you can," he explained. He actually thought this was a compliment.

I didn't.

In fact, I was so insulted that I pulled a Lucy Ricardo and decided to wear the outfit for a solid week. (No, Lucy never actually did that, but I can see her pulling something like that, can't you?)

By that time, we were seeing each other daily, and it's to Eric's credit that he didn't say a word when I answered the door every single day wearing that outfit and a sarcastic smile on my face. What he didn't know is that I dressed in other clothes all day and changed at night, right before he came over. I kept it up for a week.

Yes, I was the brattiest of brats.

But the thing is, at that time in my life—having just turned twenty, and on a steady diet of women's magazines—I had learned that you weren't supposed to dress for men. And there was no way some man was going to tell me what to wear. I was very big on my independence back then, and on controlling my own life. My response to his distaste for my clothes was really a symptom of a bigger problem, which was that I wanted to remain my own person so much that I wasn't open to any of his input on my life. At all.

And for the record, it *was* a jerky comment for him to make. But he was being honest, and if I had simply said, "Well, I like it, and that's that," then that would have been the end of it. But that wasn't my style back then. My style was to dig my heels in and prove a point, no matter what the cost.

When it comes to dressing for our husbands, I think many of us still feel that resistance. We want to steer our own ships, and sometimes all we have left is what we wear. And if we can't please ourselves or express ourselves in clothing, what else is there?

I get that, I really do. Please know that when I say "dress for him," it doesn't mean that I think our husbands should pick out our entire wardrobe.

I'm happy to say that after many seasons of dressing for everyone from boys to bosses to my peers, I've learned to dress for myself. And that is a wonderful place to be. The older I get, the less I care about what people think of me, and it's reflected in my clothing. I like feminine clothes, and I've been lovingly mocked by friends and family for wearing floral dresses a little too often. But I don't care.

I also love comfy, squishy clothes and have refused to squeeze into too-tight jeans for years. So, yeah, I dress how I want.

And this is how it should be. But I've also learned to love dressing for my husband. I like making him happy, and I like the feeling I get when he thinks I look extra cute.

If you're wondering what your clothes have to do with inner beauty, it's this:

When I wear clothes that my husband likes, and I do so because it's my heart's desire to please my husband and to make him smile, I am putting his desires before my own. And that's always a beautiful thing.

My recommendation is to have your own style, and to mix in elements that will please your husband. And once in a while, wear an outfit that is totally for him.

Don't think that I have this down and look like a modest, yet slightly desirable, fashion plate every day. *Snort!*

Four days in a row of workout clothes and messy buns still happens. It just makes my husband all the more grateful when I slip into something a little less comfortable.

I must add that, thankfully, we've both grown in wisdom and knowledge, and he'd now be mortified if I dressed in skimpy clothes outside the house. We both value modesty in a way we didn't back when we were young. (Having daughters tends to do that. Ha.)

Are you convinced that dressing for your guy is a good idea? Here are some simple ways to implement that idea.

Dressing for Him

Make a point to wear jewelry he gave you. If he went to the trouble to pick out something special for you, you should make it a point to wear it. If he's not the type to notice, you can give him a little reminder, like: *I love these earrings you got me last Christmas!*

Choose little things that he likes. Does he comment on certain things, such as a color he likes on you, or a specific top or hairstyle or dress? Whatever it is, try to work it into your rotation more often.

Proclaim your love for him in what you wear. Do you have any clothes or accessories that show you love him? Maybe a necklace with his name, or a locket with his photo? I had a *My Husband Rocks* shirt that I used to wear all the time. In fact, I wore the shirt so much that, sadly, it ripped beyond repair.

One time, I was wearing it while at an event with my husband where we met an elderly woman. She read my shirt out loud, then looked at my husband and said, "Well, good for you!" We died. Another time, I ran into an ex and I was wearing that shirt. The look on his face was priceless. He didn't exactly have to ask me what my relationship status was.

But the best thing was that my husband would always grin proudly when I wore it, even as his friends teased him that he must have bought it for me. (He didn't.) Is there something you can wear that declares your love for your husband?

Rest assured, I'm not encouraging you to spend a ridiculous amount of time worrying about what to wear. God doesn't want us to fixate on clothing. Apply these thoughts when you're getting dressed and/or when you are clothes shopping, and then go on with your day.

Your beauty should not come from outward adornment, such as elaborate hairstyles and the wearing of gold jewelry or fine clothes. Rather, it should be that of your inner self, the unfading beauty of a gentle and quiet spirit, which is of great worth in God's sight.

1 Peter 3:3–4

Reflect

Fill in this list. If you have no idea how to answer any of these questions, when it comes to your husband's preferences, ask him.

1. My husband's favorite dress is probably the _____ one.
2. My husband loves the color _____ on me.
3. The _____ is my favorite piece of jewelry from him.
4. I know he loves it when I wear my hair _____.
5. The last time we had a date, I wore _____ and I felt _____.
6. I always feel pretty when I wear _____.
7. My pajama collection could best be described as

   _____.

8. My _____ advertises my love for my husband.

If you completed a challenge today, list it here:

Day Three — Find the Good

Today, I praised God for _____ minutes.

Pray

Thank God for the many good things He put in your husband. Thank God for your husband's strong character traits, spiritual gifts, talents, and for his compatibility with you.[2]

Meditate

Read this week's verse twice out loud, then attempt to say it without looking.

Dwell

I know that God gave me the gift of _____.

Breathe

> Finally, brothers and sisters, whatever is true, whatever is noble, whatever is right, whatever is pure, whatever is lovely, whatever is admirable—if anything is excellent or praiseworthy—think about such things.
>
> Philippians 4:8

As with the rest of our lives, when it comes to our relationships, what we think is so important. God cares what is in our minds! He is the only one who knows what we're thinking, and it matters to Him. He knows us so much more intimately than anyone else.

110

And while the enemy can trick us and lie to us, he can't know our thoughts. Only God can.

And God knew that we would need reminders to keep our thoughts pure and positive. Not just to keep us from sinning against Him, but to keep us healthy and whole.

The instruction Paul gives us for thinking on good things is not only to keep our minds pure and set apart for God. He gives us this advice because it is good for us. Do you want a peaceful mind? Do you want less anxiety? Do you want to be a generally more positive person? It all starts with what we choose to think about.

Start with thanksgiving.

> Do not be anxious about anything, but in every situation, by prayer and petition, with thanksgiving, present your requests to God. And the peace of God, which transcends all understanding, will guard your hearts and your minds in Christ Jesus.
>
> Philippians 4:6–7

Train your mind to be thankful by keeping track of your thanksgivings. There is great power in writing things down. For many of us, writing something cements it in our brain. For others, reading it cements it in our brain. For plenty of us, speaking it or hearing it is the key. And for all of us, going back and reading pleasant things we've recorded reminds us of all we have to be thankful for.

Dwell on the Good in Him

What do you love about your husband? Some of you will have lists of qualities and traits that spring to mind and fill you with warm feelings. Others will stare into space and try to drum up even one thing that you love about your husband. Most of us have had days (or entire seasons) in either camp.

I remember doing this exercise for myself when I wasn't in a great place in my marriage, and after staring into space, I grudgingly wrote that my husband was a good provider. I wasn't happy with him, and it was all I was willing to concede to at the time. But when I simmered down a little and actually dwelt on it, I had to admit that, even though things weren't great between us and he was being a doodie-head, there was much to love about him.

And though I really wanted to dwell on all the things he had done wrong and the ways he had let me down, I chose to dwell on the good things. It wasn't easy. My instinct was to go back to how I'd been hurt, over and over. To relive it and take pleasure in the anger I was justified in feeling. To have imaginary conversations in the shower and make all of the good points. And, oh, what good points I can make in my head!

I wanted to think about how unfair it all was and how very right I was. Why is that so pleasurable? Going down that road is so destructive and in the end, makes us bitter, ugly people. But in the moment, it feels so good, doesn't it? Because, like Paul, no matter how well we know and desire what is right, we still desire what is wrong and bad for us. (See Romans 7:18–20.)

If we can just be strong enough to push through the temptation to dwell on all the reasons our husband angers us or irritates us or lets us down, and instead dwell on the good things God put in him . . . Oh, what beauty and peace await us on the other side!

Don't miss the key words here: the good things God put in him.

Maybe your husband is going through a truly awful season, and you just can't find anything to love about him. Maybe there is not one single moment of the day when you see good in him. But can you step back and see God in him?

Finding the God in Him

Read Psalm 139 aloud and replace the word *my* with your husband's name. Write it out if you need to.

Pray and ask God to help you see the good He put in your man.

"If any of you lacks wisdom, you should ask God, who gives generously to all without finding fault, and it will be given to you" (James 1:5).

Start with one good thing. Maybe you can't rattle off a list of beautiful things in your husband right now. That's okay. Just start with one. No matter what your situation is, you can find one good thing in your husband. Start by thanking God out loud for that, and write it down. Be faithful to dwell on this good thing when you want to dwell on the dozen negative things instead. God will bless your obedience, and over time you'll find more and more to be thankful for.

Your God loves your husband just as much as He loves you. And your God has instructed you to think on good things.

It will make you a better person. It will make you a happier, more peaceful person. If you have kids, it will make you a better mom.

And you can bet, beyond doubt, that it will make you a better wife.

Reflect

Make an acrostic poem out of your husband's name. In an acrostic poem, a letter from each word (most often the first letter) spells out another word when lined up. Here's an example, using my husband's name:

Extraordinary
Romantic
Intelligent
Courageous

You can see that it spells Eric down the side. Spell out your husband's name, using the words provided or coming up with your own. You can give this to him, or keep it as a reminder of what is good about your man.

Accepted	Joyful	Sexy
Blessed	Kind	Thoughtful
Courageous	Loved	Understanding
Delightful	Mine	Valiant
Extraordinary	Noble	Wonderfully Made
Forgiven	Original	Xtra Cute
Generous	Precious	Youthful
Handsome	Qualified	Zany
Interesting	Redeemed	

If you completed a challenge today, list it here:

Day Four — Avoid Comparison, Choose Joy

Today, I praised God for _____ minutes.

Pray

Pray that you will not be tempted to compare yourself and your husband to others. Pray that you'll have joy in all circumstances and that you will have a cheerful heart.[3]

Meditate

Copy this week's memory verse here:

_____

_____

Dwell

Other women probably wish their husband was as
_____ as mine is.

Breathe

I'll never forget the dinner party from you-know-where. We had a few couples over for dinner and games. One of the couples wasn't getting along, and everyone felt it from the moment they arrived. We tried to keep things light and cheer them up, but they just weren't having it. Things came to a head when Eric refilled my soda without my asking him to.

"Look!" the wife said, angry and pointing at me. "Eric brings Angela drinks." She turned on her husband. "How come you never do that for me?"

The chattering in the room screeched to a halt with this shrill accusation. I remember making eye contact with Eric, and saw that he was thinking the same thing as me. *Oh no.*

"Well," her husband said, "Maybe if you acted more like Angela, I *would* bring you drinks!"

That was what we jokingly referred to later as the shot heard round the world. A huge fight ensued and our fun night ended with the couple leaving, still angry at each other and undoubtedly with hurt feelings. The rest of us were in shock. Talk about awkward!

Though there were other elements at play, the detonation point was the comparisons they had made. No one wants to hear that you aren't as good a husband or wife as so and so. And while most

115

of us won't outwardly say so at a dinner party, we're all guilty of thinking or saying these things from time to time.

When it comes to comparisons wives tend to make, I see four common ones.

Comparing Him to Other Men

Whether we're doing it out loud or in our minds, comparing our husband to other men is so hurtful, and it's unfair to him, too. He doesn't need to hear about how so and so is smarter, or more fit, or better with money, or great with kids. How would you feel if he compared you to other women and found you lacking?

This goes for fictional men, too. There have been seasons in my life when I've had to stop watching certain television shows because I couldn't stop comparing my husband to the characters on the show. Though I wasn't outwardly admitting it, I was getting in a bad mood because my husband never said the things these dreamy husbands on TV said. Surely he didn't love me as much as they loved their fictional wives. And while that sounds absolutely crazy now, I don't think it's uncommon. Avoid shows and books if you find yourself feeling discontented after reading or watching them.

Comparing How He Shows Love

This is in the same vein as comparing him to other men, but it's important enough to warrant its own section. All men show love differently. While some men might effusively praise their wives publicly, others may do quiet acts of service. One might lavish gifts upon his woman, and another may bring her coffee every morning.

When Eric and I had our first baby together, he didn't bring me flowers or jewelry or anything. And I didn't let him hear the end of this for years. Other women would show off the jewelry they got for having their babies and I would get irritated all over again.

It's not as if I was a materialistic wife and just wanted things. In fact, I hadn't even considered this tradition until my baby was several months old and I heard about what some other husbands had done for their wives. Suddenly, it was a gaping hole of what my husband had not done for me.

How he was supposed to think of it when I hadn't even thought of it, I'm not sure, but I was convinced he *should* have thought of it, and I was mad that he hadn't. I felt like I mattered less and therefore I was worth less. And it really drove me crazy. Every time we went to visit a new mom and brought her flowers and gifts, I would casually remind him that *this* is what you do when you care about someone. Did I mention that I can be rather bratty?

Then one day I was talking with somebody about the first thing you eat after having a baby and how it always tastes so good because it's usually been a couple days since you had any food. And I told them about how after my daughter was born, my husband went to my favorite Mexican place and brought a burrito to me in the hospital. Halfway through my sentence, I just started laughing.

I might not have gotten a diamond bracelet or a bouquet of roses, but as anyone who knows me realizes, a burrito was even better. My husband hadn't showered me with expensive gifts, but he had taken a week off work to stay home and help out. He had driven to the pharmacy in the middle of the night when I needed something. And he had brought me that blessed burrito.

I was so loved by him, and my thoughts were just too clouded with comparison to see it. (And yes, I apologized to my husband for my attitude.)

Comparing Ourselves to Other Women

Just don't.

No good comes of this. There is no point. There will always be someone prettier, skinnier, curvier, sweeter, godlier, smarter, richer, happier, more generous, and with better hair to boot. See her blessings as just that, gifts from God. You have your own gifts from God, so let's not diminish their value by coveting what He's given to others.

Comparing Our Marriage

Although I suspect this was a problem long before social media existed, it sure does make it easier to compare your marriage to someone else's and find yours coming up short.

Just in the last month, I've seen the following on social media: A husband posted photos of an elaborate scavenger hunt he planned for his wife. A husband wrote a long, specific post about all the ways his wife sacrificed for their family. A wife shared photos of a weekend concert getaway with her in-laws, and they were all having a blast together. A wife shared photos of her couples-workout with her husband, complete with matching workout shirts. A couple went to Europe and posted gorgeous pictures. A heroic husband spontaneously went on a dangerous trip to help people in need, while his wife happily held down the fort at home.

Sometimes, scrolling through these posts, I stop and think, *What. The. Heck?*

Do people really live like this? I mean, the most exciting thing we did in the last month was go out for breakfast. And we most certainly did not wear matching shirts.

And it's not limited to social media.

A couple of years ago, we went out for an evening with another couple. The wife is a good friend of mine, and our husbands were just getting to know each other. All night, the husband was hugging and kissing his wife. He couldn't keep his hands off of her. And not in a gross or inappropriate way, just in a sweet way. She was clearly loved. And I have to admit, it made me feel a little less loved. Sure, my husband and I held hands while walking, but other than that, there wasn't much PDA going on. We were the comfy old couple and they were like newlyweds, except they weren't.

A couple of days later, I told my friend that I had almost been jealous of their lovey-dovey ways, and she darkly said, "Don't be." She then proceeded to tell me that she had found out her husband had betrayed her on the very day of our double date together. He was trying to earn her favor back by showering her with affection, and it was actually making her sick.

I felt terrible. I should have realized something was off with my friend that night, but I didn't pick up on it. Probably because I was so busy analyzing my comfy marriage and wondering why my husband didn't hang all over me anymore.

See, comparing your marriage doesn't just hurt your marriage, it keeps you from seeing more deeply into the needs of your friends and loved ones. It steals your joy and it keeps you focused on the surface, how things appear.

"Comparison is the thief of joy," as Theodore Roosevelt reportedly said, and oh, how the enemy loves to steal our joy and take our focus off the needs of those around us! And how easy it is. Just get us thinking about all the things others have that we don't have and, boom! Joy is gone. Just like that. Let's make it a little harder for him, shall we?

Choose Joy

Determine to let go of comparisons and choose joy instead. A joyful woman is a truly beautiful woman. And guess what? All of the things that increase joy in our life? We're already working on them.

Praising God, thinking good thoughts, listening to uplifting music, getting your body moving, being thankful—these are all things we've been incorporating into our days, or will be soon in the next weeks. Keep up the good work and fight the good fight. Your joy is worth it.

Not to mention how blessed your husband will be when you stop letting comparisons into your marriage.

Reflect

Have you been guilty of making unfair comparisons in your marriage? How can you avoid doing that from now on?

_____

_____

_____

_____

Of the things listed, which increases your joy most?

Praising God

Thinking good thoughts

Exercising

Listening to uplifting music

Being thankful

If you completed a challenge today, list it here:

_____

Day Five	Hand in Hand

_Today, I praised God for _____ minutes._

Pray

Pray for your husband's walk with the Lord. Pray that he will abide in Him today, that your husband will walk by the Spirit, and that the Lord would lead his steps.[4]

Meditate

Write this week's memory verse from memory:

_____

Dwell

My husband's favorite sport to play is _____.

Breathe

In simpler times, a man and woman who wanted to get to know one another would go on walks. A stroll was a chance to get away from everyone (often under the watchful eye of a chaperone who kept a respectable distance) and have a chance to talk.

Can you imagine a first date like that these days? No phones, no movies, no waiters asking what you want to order. In other words, no buffer. Nothing to do but walk, and focus on the person you're with. Sounds a little terrifying for a first date, to be honest, but long walks with my husband? Bliss.

Getting outside, away from distractions and letting my mind wander while my body moves is soothing for me. Cliché or not, long walks on the beach are my favorite, but I'll settle for a walk around my neighborhood any day of the week.

Eric and I have taken countless walks together over the years. Walks when we were young and would hold hands no matter how sweaty they got. Walks with a baby strapped to my chest. Hikes with a baby on his back. Walks while pushing heavy strollers up hills. Walks with a kid on skates, a kid on a scooter, a kid on a bike doing circles around us. Walks on the beach at night, barefoot, holding hands, and listening to the squeals of children letting the waves nip their toes.

Sometimes, we both listen to music, and the walking is something to accomplish. There are arms to pump, calories to burn, and heart rates to amp up. Sometimes there's no music, very little talking, and we hold hands until they get too sweaty and one of us finally lets go. Neither of us cares, because we're twenty years in now, and we know there's plenty of hand-holding to come.

And then sometimes, most often, we're walking and chatting. Usually one of us is chatting more than the other. (I'll let you guess which one that is.) When the kids were little, I'd often use our walks in the evening as a chance to talk about things I didn't want to talk about in front of the kids. We would make decisions as we walked. Or we would figure things out, or plan an upcoming trip.

And sometimes, I'd use our walk to air a grievance, and we would end up arguing. There is something so satisfying about pounding the pavement when you're irritated. Our heart rates were definitely amped on those walks!

For twenty years we've been walking together. A lifetime, it seems. Some seasons we didn't walk for months. Busyness, injuries, laziness, weather—one thing or another got in the way. Then, one evening after dinner, we would start back up, breathing a little harder as we got used to the hills around our house again, and feeling giddy with it all. Why did we ever quit? Why don't we do this more often? It just feels so good!

In those moments, I feel a deeper understanding of why Christians call our daily life *walking with the Lord*, and our relationship with God is often referred to as *our walk*.

Have you ever been at church and had someone ask, "How's your walk?" A new Christian might not know what that means.

It means you're in step with Him. It means you're following His path. It means you're abiding in Him, taking time to be with Him. Somewhere along the way, the phrase will likely seep into the new Christian's vocabulary. Because that's what life with God is. We're walking in Him and with Him.

For Eric and me, walking together is a tiny portion of living together. Less than a thousand hours out of hundreds of thousands of hours. But it is an immensely satisfying portion, and that's because there's something deliciously freeing about being outside and moving in the same direction. We may have to run after kids, and we may have to stop every minute to answer a toddler's questions, but we're moving, together, in the same direction. No phones. No work. No buffer.

Bliss.

When telling His followers not to be anxious, Jesus pointed to the natural world as an example of how He lovingly provides. If even the birds and flowers are taken care of, what do we need to worry about? (See Matthew 6:28–30.) If we can focus on God's provision in nature, our walks can be peaceful and help relieve anxiety.

We also know that moving our body increases endorphins, which makes us feel good and happy, which cultivates that inner beauty. So let's get moving.

Reflect

If you could take a walk anywhere in the world, where would it be and who would be with you? Describe what you might see on your walk.

_____

_____

_____

_____

_____

If you completed a challenge today, list it here: _____

Weekend Reflection

Browse some magazine headlines and list the most ridiculous ones here. How do they measure up to God's standards for beauty?

Assuming you spent time to dress for your husband at least once this week, what was his reaction? How did it make you feel?

If someone were asked to find God in you, what do you think they would find?

Was it hard to be distraction-free on your walk?

Weekly Goal Check-In

How did you do with praising God this week?

What did you learn about God as you sought new things to praise Him for?

_____

_____

_____

Will you continue the habit of praising God every day?

_____

About Bonus Weeks

I am so excited to be able to share these Bonus Weeks with you. You have persevered through four weeks of challenges, and now it's time to dig even deeper and have some fun, too.

If a Bonus Week seems like too much to take on right now, you may want to spread each one out over a couple weeks, or even a month. There's nothing wrong with taking your time and making it manageable for your life.

The two Bonus Weeks will be very similar to those you've completed, but there are some differences, too.

Longer Challenges, Deeper Goals

Each Bonus Week is centered on two overall goals, a spiritual goal and a tangible one. During Bonus Week One, we'll be cultivating contentment while also making our home a haven. You'll find five specific challenges for the week, designed so you can do one each day to work toward your goal of making your home a haven.

During Bonus Week Two, we'll be choosing selflessness while also planning an overnight date. (Don't fret if this sounds out of reach for you, there are alternatives for couples who just can't get away.) The five specific challenges for this week will help you plan an amazing time for you to connect with your husband.

Because our overall goals span the entire Bonus Week, we're not setting a smaller Weekly Goal.

No Reflect Section

You won't find any journaling questions for the Bonus Weeks. This is so you can devote more time to working on your daily challenges. You will still have a Weekend Reflection, which you can use for journaling or group discussion.

Added Content

I have included some helpful checklists and planning sheets to organize your tasks and assist you in the week-long challenges.

Let's get started with Bonus Week One!

Cultivating Contentment While Making Your Home a Haven

This week we are going to work on growing contented hearts and minds as we seek to make our homes a haven.

What does one have to do with the other? When we have learned the secret to being content in any circumstances, our homes will become much happier places. Tackling the hands-on jobs that need to be done, while also working on your heart, means you and your husband (along with the rest of your family) will be doubly blessed.

As we work through the challenges and daily reading this week there are lots of small steps to take. Along with doing fun things like adding romance to your bedroom, you will also be doing some cleaning (not so fun, but you'll be glad you did).

When you get to the Weekend Reflection, you will find a Home Evaluation. This is the culmination of all of your work. You will be able to sit down in a welcoming, clean space, go through the checklist, and congratulate yourself on a job well done. You will also find a few reflection questions for journaling or group discussion.

Three Ways to Make Your Home a Haven

When you think of a haven, what comes to mind? The house you grew up in? A special place you love to visit? Here are three basic steps toward making your home a peaceful refuge for your family.

Foster Acceptance

Everyone wants to feel like they belong somewhere in the world. Don't we want our families to feel they belong at home? For me, this is the most important part of making a home. Yes, we want to practice kindness and patience, and we want to create a cheerful atmosphere, but we're all going to fall short of those things on some days. We'll have our cranky days when we're not as patient, and we'll have moody days when kindness doesn't come easily.

But if we have built a foundation of acceptance, and our loved ones know that no matter what happens, no matter what they do, they belong and they're safe, then we've already made huge strides toward creating a haven.

This means everyone gets a clean slate every morning. It means you're always welcomed and loved. It means no silent treatments, no freezing each other out. It means lots of hugs and kisses. It means no hurtful teasing. We love to tease in our family, but we do it in a light, fun way. If it starts to hit below the belt or turn personal, that is meanness, not teasing.

Maintain a Clean Environment

A clean space is always more welcoming and peaceful than a dirty or messy one. Your house doesn't need to be spotless, or museum worthy, but it should be clean and at least somewhat tidy.

If you're regularly late because you can't find things, or if allergies are made worse due to dust and dirt, no one in your home can be at peace. The challenges this week will help you create a clean home.

Celebrate Your Family

Your home is the perfect place to celebrate your family. We all know that person who is a huge fan of something or someone, so much so that their house is filled with photos, decorations, books and such that show their dedication to the sports team, celebrity, musician, etc.

Let's be fans of our families.

Put up photos of happy times, embrace your heritage and cook meals that reflect it, display memorabilia from family vacations or outings, display your children's artwork, watch old family movies together.

When your family comes home, they will be greeted by reminders that this is their home and that they belong here.

Imagine Your Ideal

Day One

If you want to work on creating a welcoming haven, I recommend writing down three to five words that describe how you'd like your home to be. I call them your *home words*. Think about what you want your home to say, how you want it to feel, and sum it up in a few words. You might choose words like *sanctuary*, *refuge*, *warm*, *welcoming*, *cheerful*, *clean*, *bright*, *peaceful*—whatever words capture your ideal home. Then, write those words on a piece of paper or an index card and put it where you'll see it every day. Let it serve as a reminder of what you are trying to create.

Write out a few words you would like associated with your home.

_____

This process will be radically different for each of you. Depending on your personality—and perhaps, more important, how you were raised—overhauling your home may be extraordinarily easy or discouragingly difficult.

Start small with the steps listed here, and over time, you *will* make significant changes. I am a self-proclaimed former slob. If I can do this, you can. There are still times when my free spirit takes over and my house becomes a disaster zone. But when I get things back in order, I always feel content and peaceful.

In addition to dealing with our own shortcomings, most of our families probably are not going to jump up and down with excitement when we start changing things up. If you encounter some resistance, tackle any backlash with prayer and consistency. Model a good attitude and persevere. I have no doubt that you can change the environment in *most* of your home . . . even if your teenager's bedroom never quite gets there.

Give yourself grace, and extend that grace to the other people in your home. You can't build a house overnight, and you can't build a home overnight. So stay committed to working on it, but don't forget to have fun along the way.

Memory Verse

> A wise woman builds her house, but with her own hands
> the foolish one tears hers down.
> Proverbs 14:1

Write this week's memory verse on a sticky note or index card and post it on your bathroom mirror or wherever you'll see it often.

Bonus Week One Challenges

Challenges in this Bonus Week are a little different. Each challenge has a few steps instead of one little thing. If you feel overwhelmed, just do one day's reading and one challenge each week, and take a full five weeks to complete Bonus Week One.

If your life is especially busy right now, or your house is officially a disaster zone, I recommend taking the slower approach. It will be worth it, and you won't lose your mind in the process.

Day One: Turn Your Bedroom into Romance Central #byhromancecentral

1. Clean your bedroom, using the checklist on page 137.
2. Clutter isn't relaxing, so be sure not to skip this step. Clear out any clutter and tidy up. Get rid of any of your kids' toys, or store them in a covered box if you must keep them in the room.
3. Add romantic elements: candles, flowers, photos of your wedding or honeymoon.
4. Personalize your space. In addition to the photos, add mementos, signs, artwork, or personalized pillows or throws. We have a sign that says, "Always kiss me goodnight." My daughter has pillows on her bed that say, "Mr." and "Mrs." You could display a large letter for your last name (found at most home decorating stores) or a canvas print with lyrics of your song or a special Bible verse. Anything that adds a personal touch and makes the room feel like a special getaway just for you two.
5. Make sure the room smells nice and fresh. Cleanliness alone is a great smell, but you could also get a scented candle or some lavender sheet spray. I like to use different scents in our bedroom than I do in the rest of the house. My favorite is a

black scented candle that smells to me like men's cologne. It's masculine and sexy, and definitely gives the bedroom a different vibe than the sweet smells I use elsewhere.

Day Two: The Heart of the Home #byhheartofmyhome

For many of us, the kitchen is the heart of the home. It's where we prepare foods that will nourish our families, and oftentimes where everyone gathers or hovers about as we're preparing and cooking.

1. Let's work on making the kitchen an inviting space. Allow family members to help with cooking, even if they don't do things the same way you would. Get help with cleaning, and teach them to take care of their messes, but try not to alienate loved ones by insisting everything be perfect.

2. If you don't already have a meal-planning system in place, consider creating one. Even if you just keep the ingredients for a few go-to dinners on hand, you'll increase the peace in your household. What Margaret Kim Peterson wrote in *Keeping House* resonated with me when I read it during a particularly busy season of life: "In too many households, the need of people for an evening meal has become a perpetual emergency."[1]

   At that time, I found myself surprised that dinnertime arrived on a nightly basis, and as a result we were eating too much fast food. Making grocery shopping and meal planning a priority helped tremendously. You will find meal-planning helps in the online content at angelamillsbooks.com/husbandbonuscontent.

3. Add homey elements to your kitchen: favorite cookbooks, a cookie jar that is filled often, fresh flowers by the sink, bowls of produce for easy snacks, cute photos or kids' artwork on the fridge.

4. Clean your kitchen using the checklist on page 137–138.

Day Three: Living Areas and Bathroom #byhmakingahaven

We're going to address making living areas cozy on Day Five. As for your bathrooms, you'll want to give them a good scrubbing. Today there are not a lot of fun elements to add; we're just going to focus on getting these areas nice and clean. If both your living areas and bathrooms are going to be a big ordeal, spread this out over a couple of days.

1. Clean your living areas, using the checklist on page 138.
2. Clean your bathrooms, using the checklist.

Day Four: A System in Place #byhorganizing

Now that you've cleaned the main areas of the home, you'll need a system for keeping things clean and tidy.

1. Set aside a few hours one day a week to clean the whole house. If you work all week, do this on the weekend and ask the family to pitch in. Many hands make light work. Reward everyone afterward with something like a fun game, a bike ride, or a movie night.

   Alternatively, set aside forty-five minutes or so each day for weekly cleaning, and tackle a different room each day. I've used the weekly approach and the daily method, and they've both worked well in different seasons in my life. Check out the online content at angelamillsbooks.com/husbandbonuscontent for printable charts and more helps with housekeeping.

2. In addition to weekly cleaning, you'll want to spend a little time each day on daily cleaning. Make beds, do laundry, wash dishes, take out the trash, wipe down sinks and counters; these are just a few things you'll want to do each day. Find a time that works best for you, and if you have kids, get them

involved as soon as possible. Even toddlers can pick up their toys. (You'll find daily cleaning lists in the online content, too.)

3. Create a drop-everything spot for each person in the family. If that's too overwhelming right now, at least make one for your husband. It will make his day, and yours, so much easier. A simple fabric bin, a basket, a tray, or a men's valet will work. He can place in it his wallet, keys, phone, and anything else he needs on a daily basis. This also helps if you have kids and their stuff tends to take over the house. Keeping an area for your husband's necessities will make getting out the door each morning a little easier.

    For kids, try creating cubbies or a shelf in a closet where they can dump backpacks, sports equipment, instruments, etc. so they can grab everything they need in the morning. And don't forget to create a spot for yourself.

4. Pick a spot for mail and papers, and develop a system for reducing clutter. We have a recycling bin in our garage, right outside the door that goes into our house. Then, inside, I have a couple of places for mail. My husband handles our bills and finances, so everything of that nature goes into a basket for him to take when he's ready. The rest of the household mail goes into a box for me to deal with. Grocery or restaurant coupons I think I might use are clipped and stashed in my wallet right away. (Except for when they aren't, and then they sit on the kitchen counter until they expire.)

5. Spend ten minutes a day dealing with clutter. Even if you only hit this goal three times a week, you can keep your whole house fairly clutter-free. Make a checklist of all of the areas prone to clutter, and spend a few minutes each day working your way through them. For instance, our kitchen junk drawer, our media cabinet, and my nightstand drawers are areas I regularly need to attack.

6. Every night before bed, spend fifteen minutes picking up, wiping down counters, and getting things ready for the next

day. My girls and I joke that we get more done in the fifteen minutes before someone comes over than we do all week. In the evenings, I try to summon the energy to clean up like someone is coming over. Even if you can manage five minutes, your mornings will be so much nicer.

Day Five: A Coziness Check #byhhygge

1. Pray-walk around your house. Pray as you go from room to room, thanking God and asking Him to bless your family as you do.

2. Read Day Five and use the Coziness Check on page 158–159 to evaluate your home. I recommend doing this in a comfy chair with a cup of tea. Take notes and plan which suggestions you can implement in your home.

Household Cleanup Checklist

Bedroom
- ☐ Remove clutter
- ☐ Dust all surfaces and polish wood furniture
- ☐ Change sheets
- ☐ Make bed
- ☐ Vacuum or mop
- ☐ Clean mirrors and windows
- ☐ Clean windowsills

Kitchen
- ☐ Clear clutter
- ☐ Clean surfaces and appliances
- ☐ Do dishes or load dishwasher

- ☐ Clean counters
- ☐ Sweep and mop floors
- ☐ Clean out fridge and wipe down shelves
- ☐ Clean fronts of cabinets
- ☐ Clean sink
- ☐ Switch out hand towels

Living Areas

- ☐ Pick up clutter and straighten up
- ☐ Dust all surfaces
- ☐ Vacuum or sweep and mop
- ☐ Vacuum furniture
- ☐ Polish wood furniture
- ☐ Clean windows and windowsills
- ☐ Put a fresh tablecloth or runner on dining table

Bathrooms

- ☐ Scrub shower and tub
- ☐ Clean toilets
- ☐ Clean mirrors
- ☐ Sweep and mop floors
- ☐ Take out trash
- ☐ Stock paper goods
- ☐ Switch out hand towels

Stop Complaining

Day Two

Pray

Pray that you will have a content heart and that God will bless you as you focus on what is excellent and praiseworthy. Pray that you will be a blessing to your husband.[2]

Meditate

As you look at your memory verse today, highlight or underline the verse in your Bible. Read Titus 2:3–5 and/or other verses for homemakers.

Dwell

My husband's strongest character trait is

_____

_____

Breathe

I've done each of the challenges in this book. I tend to gravitate toward the tangible, hands-on challenges, but it's the heart challenges that wind up being the most impactful. And, wow, has my marriage been blessed when I intentionally work on being a pleasant, respectful wife.

I also know that I need to redo these kinds of challenges over and over as the years go by, because I'm stubborn in my ways and find myself reverting back to a complaining, disrespectful woman when I'm moody, tired, or hangry (hungry + angry = hangry). My family could tell you some crazy tales about times when I went so long without eating that I practically bit their heads off over insignificant things.

Now we've come to the heart-challenge I've been struggling with most lately. Complaining. I never used to be a big complainer at all. In fact, if anything, I was such a Pollyanna, always looking on the bright side, that it drove some people crazy. (I know this because they told me so. You gotta love honest people.)

But just when you start to think something isn't *your* issue, you find out that maybe it could be. The last few years have been hard on me physically. I've had some health issues, surgeries, and hormonal problems that have been difficult to work through. One of the results of these circumstances is that I've found myself complaining more than ever before.

It started with the health problems. As much as I was trying to *Pollyanna* this, complaining became my go-to. *I'm hot, I'm tired, I'm in pain. Ugh.*

Then, it was my situation. *It stinks that I can't work out like I used to. It stinks that I can't lose weight. It stinks that I can't even function like I used to. Ugh, ugh.*

Next came the people in my life. *Everyone is so annoying! No one understands! People are the worst! Ugh, ugh, ugh!*

Just reading this now makes me cringe. After spending some time in God's Word and being convicted to the point of crying, I knew something had to change. Once I realized how unpleasant I had become, I prayed and resolved to be more positive. And by keeping track of my blessings, praising God more often, and yes, focusing on what was good, I was able to cut back on the complaining.

But instead of going back to my usual the-glass-is-half-full self, it now took real work to tame my complaining tongue. The instinct to be discontent and unpleasant still lingers in me. It's something I have to stay on top of or I'll slide right back into that cringe-worthy person I was becoming before.

How to Stop Grumbling

Philippians 2:14 commands us to "do everything without grumbling." It's safe to say that God does not want us to complain, and in the Bible He gives us keys for how to avoid becoming complainers.

In Philippians 4, we find that thankfulness breeds contentment, and it's pretty hard to complain when you're thinking of all the blessings in your life. And if you can read this book, trust me, you've got a fountain of blessings and advantages that many would love to have.

A Physical Reminder

A few years ago, a Kansas City church gave away purple bracelets that were to remind wearers to stop complaining. The idea was to wear the bracelet on one wrist and when you caught yourself complaining, switch it to the other wrist. The goal was to go twenty-one days without complaining and having to switch the bracelet. The pastor who invented the challenge, Will Bowen, said it took him three months to complete twenty-one days, and that some people took up to seven months before they could go three solid weeks without complaining.[3]

Judging by the more than eleven million bracelets they've distributed upon request,[4] it's easy to see that complaining is a widespread problem.

Perhaps you could try something like this and wear a physical reminder to stop complaining. Doing so might help you obey God's Word and stop grumbling, and that's always worth it.

Replace Complaints with Thanks

Today, focus on replacing complaining thoughts with thankful thoughts, for "out of the overflow of the heart, the mouth speaks" (Luke 6:45 BSB). If you're dwelling on thankful things, that is what will come out of your mouth instead of complaints, and you'll be a more pleasant person and wife.

The section below will help with this. In one column, you'll list your complaints. Go ahead, don't hold back. Get everything, and I mean *everything*, off your chest. Light that column up! Then, in the next column, write a thankful thought to replace it. Here's an example:

Complaint:

The dishes are a never-ending cycle and I'm the only one who does them!

Thanksgiving:

We are blessed to have plenty of food to eat and clean, pretty dishes to use!

Complaint:	Thanksgiving:

If you completed a challenge today, list it here:

Content with Him

Pray

Pray that you will be content in all circumstances, and thank God that you can do all things through Christ who strengthens you.[5]

Meditate

Read this week's verse twice out loud, then attempt to say it without looking.

Dwell

My strongest character trait is_____.

Breathe

We've learned to avoid comparing, to focus on the good, and to reminisce wisely. All of these things help move us toward being content with the husband God gave us.

But reaching contentment isn't a one-time achievement. Like any godly trait, contentment is a condition of the heart that needs to be nurtured.

Nothing stays the same in life except God and His Word. In fact, one thing we can be certain of is that everything else changes.

Your circumstances will change. Will you still be content when you have to move away from family or quit your job or go back to work?

Your relationships will change. Will you still be content when the exciting days have passed and you're in a comfy rut, or when your husband suddenly has to work long hours and is never home?

Your lifestyle will change. Will you still be content when you have to cut back financially, or deal with the stress of sudden chaos and busyness?

Your husband will change. Will you still be content when your cheerful husband goes through a deep depression or when your faithful groom admits he is struggling with lust?

You will change. Will you still be content when your dreams are crushed and life doesn't look like you thought it would?

We are not guaranteed an easy, happy life. We are guaranteed trials and suffering. We are guaranteed a strong and faithful God.

The only thing that never changes is God and His Word.

> I the LORD do not change.
>
> Malachi 3:6

The secret to being content with your husband is being content with God's love for you. Whatever you're not getting from your husband, you will get from God. After eighteen years of marriage, I can absolutely say that I am thankful for my husband's shortcomings, as they've brought me closer to God.

I like to focus on the positive, but for now, let's address the negatives you may be feeling about your husband. How does God fill in the gaps where you're missing something from your man?

Do you feel your husband doesn't appreciate you? Well, God sees all you do and all you don't do, and loves you either way. "Your Father, who sees what is done in secret, will reward you" (Matthew 6:18).

Do you feel unloved? God loves you so much more completely than any human ever could. "The Lord appeared to us in the past, saying: 'I have loved you with an everlasting love; I have drawn you with unfailing kindness'" (Jeremiah 31:3).

Does your husband not satisfy you? Only God can truly satisfy you! "Then Jesus declared, 'I am the bread of life. Whoever comes to me will never go hungry, and whoever believes in me will never be thirsty'" (John 16:35).

Does your husband not support your dreams? God put those dreams in your heart, and when you submit to His will, He will make good on your dreams in His time, or He'll change them to suit His plans. "Take delight in the Lord, and he will give you the desires of your heart" (Psalm 37:4).

Is your husband lacking as a spiritual leader? We have the ultimate spiritual leader in Jesus. "You call me 'Teacher' and 'Lord,' and rightly so, for that is what I am" (John 13:13).

Don't Compare Him to God

Well, duh, you're thinking, right? *Of course we're not comparing our husbands to the Lord!* But, hold on. Maybe we are sometimes. When we expect our husbands to be everything to us and to be, well, kind of perfect, aren't we expecting things of him that we can only expect of God? Only God can love us perfectly. Our men will always mess up, and for that matter, so will we. Don't expect your husband to take on the roles only God can fulfill in your life. He can't and shouldn't be your everything.

Next time you're feeling the weight of whatever your husband is lacking, strive to rest in the true contentment that only comes from trusting God. You don't have to carry that burden! Give it to God in prayer. Your heart will be at peace, and your husband will be blessed for having a content wife.

If you completed a challenge today, list it here:

Day Four — Content with Our Means

Pray

Pray that you and your husband will be good stewards of what God has given you. Pray for your husband to have wisdom for your finances, and that you will not develop a love of money.[6]

Meditate

Copy this week's memory verse here:

_____

_____

_____

Dwell

If money were no object, I'd buy my husband a

_____

Breathe

You may have guessed by now that I'm an _I Love Lucy_ fan. She's not exactly a model wife, what with her scheming and lying and jealous attitudes. But I can't help it—I adore her lovably bratty ways. Maybe because she represents that little bit of the brat in all of us.

In one episode, Lucy went to a home show featuring brand-new furniture. We see her coming home and viewing her small apartment in a new light. She walks into the room with a dissatisfied sigh, lets out one of her patented _Ugh_s and then begins

146

complaining about everything in the room with a scowl on her face. It isn't long before she's refusing to sit on her "repulsive" furniture. It's funny because we can relate.

Have you ever come home from a model home or a friend's house and found your own home lacking? I know I have.

As we work on making our homes a haven this week, let's make sure we aren't comparing our homes with what someone else has, and that we're doing this job with a heart of contentment. It won't matter how clean and beautiful our home is if we have a heart full of ugly discontentment.

I remember hearing a message a few years ago about credit cards.

Something from that message has stuck with me to this day. The speaker said the reason credit card debt is so high in our country is because most people want to live above their means, and credit cards made it easy to do so. She then pointed out that we should try to live within or below our means to stay out of debt.

It was a simple concept, and one I should already have figured out by that point of my life. We had amassed some credit card debt, so I wondered what living within our means would actually look like. After putting pen to paper and working it out, I realized it would look a lot like telling myself no a lot more often. How simple. And yet it was harder than I thought. I quickly decided making more money was the answer, and I drove myself crazy for a while, trying to earn enough to be able to say yes as often as I'd like. At the time, my husband didn't support the idea of my working outside the home, but I would still look for jobs and come up with schemes for how I could manage it while homeschooling our kids. Eventually, I always came to my senses and decided to respect my husband's wishes and just do a better job budgeting. And then, a few months later, I'd be in the same spot, longing for more and trying to make it work.

I had a lot to learn about living within my means, and it wasn't until I was reading Philippians a few years later that I realized my true problem wasn't financial at all.

147

I am not saying this because I am in need, for I have learned to be content whatever the circumstances. I know what it is to be in need, and I know what it is to have plenty. I have learned the secret of being content in any and every situation, whether well fed or hungry, whether living in plenty or in want. I can do all this through him who gives me strength.

Philippians 4:11–13

Paul says that he's learned the secret of being content. It should make your ears perk up when you read in the Bible that someone has learned the secret to something. I know it did mine, back in my days of financial frustration. The secret wasn't in making more money, or having a better budget. The secret was in trusting that God will give you the strength you need, no matter what your circumstances are.

The secret is that it has nothing at all to do with your efforts, or your income. What a relief! Of course, we're still responsible for being good stewards of what God gives us, and it makes sense to follow a budget.

You can be content, because God's got this.

One of the few times that it can be good to compare yourself with others is when you're feeling dissatisfied with your home or your income. Take a minute to compare it to someone who has less than you, not to feel superior, but to remind yourself of how little you have to complain about.

My stepmom, Debby, taught me a valuable lesson in this. When my husband and I were younger, and we were living on very little money, my parents would bless my young kids with presents we couldn't afford. I was looking through a catalog from a popular toy company, and the prices were staggering. "I wouldn't even spend this kind of money if I did have it!" I exclaimed. I didn't want them spoiling my daughter with one of these expensive gifts. And, more truthfully, it bothered me that we couldn't provide this longed-for item, but they could.

I went on a bit about how ridiculous it was that people spent that kind of money on toys.

"Well," Debby said, "it's all relative. If you had more money, this wouldn't seem like much at all to you. Just like what you spend on gifts probably seems excessive to someone with far less money."

Though she wasn't trying to shame me, her point drove home. I knew, and even saw firsthand from going on mission trips, that there were plenty of people who had far less, if anything, to spend on Christmas gifts. The budget we had for gifts would seem astronomical to them, when they were just trying to put food on the table. And I knew the true meaning of Christmas that I drilled into my kids every year. But somewhere along the way, I had allowed that to slip my mind and here I was, stressing about something as unimportant as buying gifts.

Even when we know better, longing and coveting can sneak into our hearts so easily. When your friend posts photos of their European vacation and you start to research how much plane tickets would cost. When the Pottery Barn catalog comes and you realize how very shabby and not at all chic your couches are. When your sister's pantry is stocked with all organic, GMO-free, gluten-free foods and you are down to two boxes of macaroni and cheese until payday.

When the woman in front of you at church is decked out in the latest fashions and you're wearing your trusty old go-to dress. Again.

Whether the burden of financially providing for your family falls on you, your husband, or both of you, it will make a huge impact when you decide to be content with what you have. How pleasant our homes will be when we aren't longing for newer furniture or a bigger house. How happy our outings will be when we aren't wishing for something better to do. How successful you and your husband will feel when you commit to not complaining about your budget.

Don't think that people with more money than you are exempt from these struggles. Like Debby said, it's all relative. Money problems can happen no matter what your income is. Some of the richest and most powerful people in the world are still scheming and hoarding and striving for more and more.

If you're not content in your heart, there will never be an income level you reach that allows you to rest and say, "We've made it. I long for nothing."

Because it's not the amount of money, security, or things, that give you that unexplainable peace or contentment.

It's the trust in a merciful, generous God that supplies all of our needs.

Hebrews 13:5 tells us, "Keep your lives free from the love of money and be content with what you have, because God has said, 'Never will I leave you; never will I forsake you.'"

Here, we read that we're to be content with what we have *because* God has said He'll never leave us. When we're wanting more, we need to pause and remember, God is enough.

Consider also what Jesus says in Luke 12:15: "Then he said to them, 'Watch out! Be on your guard against all kinds of greed; life does not consist in an abundance of possessions.'"

Practical Ways to Be Content with Your Means

Cancel catalogs and emails that make you want to spend money unnecessarily. When you actually need something, you will know what stores to check. You don't need daily or weekly reminders of available products. This goes for clothes, home decor, makeup, or whatever appeals to you. As a homeschool mom, I had to stop looking through curriculum catalogs all year, because I was always finding new curriculum I felt I had to have, when in fact, I already had plenty.

Make the most of what you do have. If you're longing for a large house, spend some time making your house warm and inviting, thanking God for your home as you work. If you can't travel to exotic places like your neighbors do every summer, find an affordable, local outing and be determined to enjoy the people you're with. If you're sick of wearing the same clothes all of the time, mix things up and create new outfits from what you already have.

Take a social media break. If you're regularly feeling jealous or longing for more than you have when you go on social media, take a break from it. Better to cut that out of your life than to slip into a discontented state. And can we all just acknowledge the superficial aspect of social media? The majority of people only post about their great moments. So don't compare their greatest moments with the humdrum of your everyday life.

Reach out to others. Giving time and energy to others can help you be content with your means. You won't have the time to worry about yourself when you're helping someone else.

Donate to trusted charities that serve the less fortunate. Serve with a local food ministry or a loft house ministry. Go on a local or short-term mission trip. Sponsor a child with Compassion International and write them letters. When we start to give to others, our wants become less as their needs become more.

Let's be wives who are content with what the Lord has given us and where He has placed us. In doing so, we're well on our way to making our homes a restful haven.

If you completed a challenge today, list it here:

Creating Coziness

Day Five

Pray

Pray that you will be a wise woman who builds her home, and that God will lead you as you create a haven for your family.[7]

Meditate

Write this week's memory verse from memory:

_____

Dwell

Our home could best be described as _____.

No matter what your preferred decorating style is, everyone wants a home base that feels cozy. Lately, I've been studying—and loving—the concept of _hygge_ (pronounced hoo-ga or hue-gah). _Hygge_ is a Scandinavian word that has no exact English translation, but has to do with experiencing the feeling of coziness. A quick look into _hygge_ points to many elements that create this cozy feeling, and you'll find lists on how to create _hygge_ by using everything from candles to warm drinks and crackling fires to just plain old togetherness. But the true feeling of _hygge_ has more to it.

In _The Little Book of Hygge_, Meik Wiking says,

> Hygge is about an atmosphere and an experience, rather than about things. It is about being with the people we love. A feeling of home. A feeling that we are safe, that we are shielded from the world and allow ourselves to let our guard down.[8]

Can you see why I love the idea of _hygge_?

A true sense of welcoming will come from the hearts of those in the home, and especially from those who run the home, namely you.

So while it may not be possible to light a dozen candles and snuggle on the sofa with a cup of tea every afternoon, it is possible to create a cozy feeling of welcome. A place that makes everyone feel as if they belong, and most important, to feel safe.

Today, we're going to look at some ways to create coziness in your home, both physical and emotional.

Emotional Coziness: Creating a Safe Home Base

Creating a cozy home base starts with protecting the hearts of our family members. Our actions and words go a long way toward making those we love feel safe and welcome.

Be Accepting

Don't forget what we covered on Day One this week. It is so important to foster acceptance, and that starts with you. What a lovely environment you'll be creating for your family when they know they belong.

Be Cheerful

> A gentle answer turns away wrath,
> but a harsh word stirs up anger.
> Proverbs 15:1

Monitoring your tone of voice can do so much to improve the atmosphere in your home. Strive to give gentle answers and create an ambience of cheerfulness. I've heard that it's impossible to answer the phone and sound upset when you have a smile on your face, and I've found it to be true. Try this at home, too. "A cheerful heart is good medicine, but a crushed spirit dries up the bones" (Proverbs 17:22). Be cheerful!

Be Interested

I can't stress this enough. It's no fun to feel like no one cares about your day, your interests, or how you spend your time. Be the person who is interested in your husband's and children's day. We're going to talk more about this next week, but keep it in mind for now.

Be Pleasant

In addition to being cheerful, be pleasant. Don't save your best manners for everyone else; use them at home, too. Set an example of kindness, and remember that a little bit of patience makes everyone's day better. "Be kind and compassionate to one another, forgiving each other, just as in Christ, God forgave you" (Ephesians 4:32).

Show Respect

We hear a lot about respecting our husbands, but let's show basic respect to everyone in our homes. Realize that each person is an individual created by God for a purpose, and show them the same respect you would show a stranger or colleague.

If you knew you were going home to a place every day where you would be greeted cheerfully, asked about your day, treated with respect and kindness, wouldn't you just love going home? Don't we want our families to feel the same way?

Environmental Coziness: Creating a Pleasant Refuge

In addition to emotional changes we can make, there are plenty of tangible things we can do to make our homes feel cozier. This week, as we're wrapping up our challenges, look with new eyes at the places your family gathers. See if you can add some of these cozy elements over the next few weeks.

A Clean Environment

We're working on this all week with our challenges, so I'm not going to say much more here. Just this: a clean environment helps almost everyone to feel more centered, safe, and at peace.

Bring Nature Indoors

Being in beautiful places in nature really promotes peace in our heart. So bring some nature inside. Plants and flowers not only help purify the air, they go a long way in cheering up the room. That's why we bring them to someone who is in the hospital or a care center. Don't miss the opportunity to add peaceful vibes to your own home with plants. A beautifully decorated room becomes cozy with the addition of a big bouquet of flowers or a leafy green plant.

Promote Comfort

If you don't already have an area where everyone can feel comfortable without worrying too much about mussing things, consider creating a spot like this. Make sure you have soft throws and pillows for snuggling, and the kind of couch or chair someone can curl up on comfortably without fear of messing it up.

Candles and Lighting

Candlelight is soft and warm and signals the brain that it's time to settle down. In the same way, low lighting is super cozy for evenings at home. Use lamps and dimmers to transition into evening lighting and create a homey feeling. If candles aren't allowed or practical in your area, battery-operated ones work just as well.

Homey Aromas

Everyone's idea of homey aromas differs, depending on what they grew up with. I love the smell of baked goods fresh from the oven in the fall and winter. In summer, I prefer clean, crisp smells such as lemon, or beachy smells like coconut. I think when my kids are grown, they'll associate the smell of snickerdoodles with home, as I make this favorite cookie often. Whatever your preferred scents are, use them liberally, with scented candles, essential oils, or simmering pots on the stove.

Games

Keep some board games or card games on hand, and play them often. Or, do challenging puzzles together as a family. You'll be creating an atmosphere of fun and making some great family memories.

Books

As a writer and avid reader, I may be biased on this, but I do believe that books lend a certain amount of coziness to a space. I love being surrounded by big shelves teeming with books, but even a stack of a few favorites can add a great deal of charm to a room. Keep your husband's and kids' favorite books out for easy access.

Celebrate Your Family

Remember on Day One when we talked about being a fan of your family? Don't forget to add photos and mementos that will remind you all of happy times.

Mark the Seasons

We have home decor that we change out with the seasons. Sometimes it's just different throw pillows, or new scented candles. Time passes quickly, as we all know, so it's nice to acknowledge the seasons and that you're all passing that time together.

Make Your Family's Favorite Foods

Everyone feels loved when you remember their favorite food and prepare it for them. Not only will your house smell delicious, you'll be creating a cozy dinnertime and blessing your family members. You don't have to do this every night. Even if you rotate through one family member's favorite foods each month, you'll be doing great. When I'm making my grocery lists, I'll often ask my husband or kids if there's anything they'd like for dinner in the next week. It's an easy way to show them I care.

Traditions, Routines, and Rituals

I'm a big believer in traditions. Add a few traditions your family can look forward to every year. Keep it simple—they don't have to be anything extravagant. One of our favorite traditions is making

Irish soda bread for St. Patrick's Day. It's just a small thing, but you'd better believe that my kids aren't going to let St. Patrick's Day pass without that soda bread!

In addition to traditions, establish routines and rituals. Tuck your kids in every night and pray with them or sing to them. Celebrate small accomplishments, like an improved grade or a job promotion—and for the little ones: potty training.

Have rituals for when someone is sick—offering a certain soup or tea or just making a bed on the couch and watching *I Love Lucy* reruns together. That's what my mom used to do for us when we were sick, which may explain why I mention Lucy so much in this book.

Creating Coziness on a Budget

If you don't have the funds to buy plush throw pillows and gallery photo frames, don't worry. There are many budget-friendly options available.

Candles are amazing, and you can find them at the dollar store. Instead of flowers, buy an inexpensive plant that will last longer. You don't need expensive frames to put family photos up; use magnets for the fridge, or scotch tape. Ask grandparents for board games for Christmas, or visit yard sales and thrift stores.

When our kids were younger, one of our favorite spaces in our house was our seasonal table. We would find things on walks or in our backyard and display them on a small table. Depending on the season, we'd have stones, or leaves, or acorns or pinecones, dried flowers, or even seasonal crafts the kids made. And it was totally free.

When it comes to decorating, use Pinterest to find DIY versions of styles you love. Pinterest can be a double-edged sword, making us feel inadequate if our homes aren't perfect like most of the photos shared there. But there are also so many useful hacks for finding something beautiful and expensive and making it for a few dollars. So, use it with caution and remember to avoid comparisons.

I hope you're inspired to kick up the coziness a notch in your own home. Next, you'll find a Coziness Check to help get you started.

Don't be overwhelmed by this list. It is a lot for one wife to tackle. Instead, see it as something to accomplish over time, maybe even taking months or a full year to put all of these ideas into practice. (As I'm writing this, we haven't even fully unpacked from a move yet, so there is not one family photo gracing my walls. It'll take time to create a cozy home out of our new house, and it may take time for you, too.) Give yourself grace.

If you completed a challenge today, list it here:

Coziness Check

Creating an Emotionally Safe Haven:

- Foster acceptance
- Be cheerful
- Be interested
- Be pleasant
- Show respect

Elements for a Physically Pleasing Haven:

- Plants and/or flowers
- Comfy area that can be mussed
- Throw pillows
- Throw blankets
- Candles
- Varied lighting
- Family photos
- Mementos of happy times

- Well-loved books
- Games and puzzles

Things to Do:
- Create a clean environment
- Create homey aromas
- Mark the seasons
- Make favorite foods

Traditions, Routines, and Rituals to Implement:
- Bedtime routines
- Holiday traditions
- Sick-day rituals
- Celebrate small (and big) accomplishments

Weekend Reflection

Does your house show that you're a fan of your family? What touches have you added?

_____

_____

_____

_____

_____

What were your home words?

_____

_____

_____

_____

What can you tangibly do to make these words a reality?

_____

_____

_____

How did you work on creating emotional coziness this week?

_____

_____

_____

Have you been able to replace your complaints with thanksgiving this week? How so?

_____

_____

How have you worked on being content with your means?

_____

_____

_____

Choosing Selflessness While Planning an Overnight Date

We do not live in a culture that celebrates selflessness. How often have you heard, "Find yourself," "Please yourself," or "You're number one"?

And yet Christians are admonished to do exactly the opposite and "value others above yourselves" (Philippians 2:3).

This week, we'll dig into a few areas where we as wives can choose to be selfless in our everyday life. Sometimes it's easier to be selfless in the big moments. Not because it's ever easy, exactly, but because the major things in life tend to bring on more discussion and thought. And when we've been growing in God, we can make those big decisions wisely and selflessly.

But in the monotony of day-to-day events, it's harder to remember to be selfless. Especially when it's three in the morning and your toddler just threw up.

As we work on developing a selfless attitude in our hearts, we'll also be planning an overnight date for our husbands. If this seems impossible, don't quit just yet. I'll have some options for those of you who can't leave the house. I'm confident we'll find a way to make it work for you, so keep reading.

Day One — A Reward for You Too

If you're wondering why I've coupled these themes of being selfless with planning a special date, it's because our focus for most of this book has been on the ordinary moments in our day-to-day life. I thought it would be fun to end with something out of the ordinary, something that can be the culmination of all of your hard work, and something that you don't get to do every day. And we'll have lots of opportunities to be selfless while planning this date.

This week's overall challenge is going to be a lot less labor intensive than last week's. And in my opinion, a lot more fun.

This challenge isn't just going to bless your husband's socks off, but is a sweet reward for you, too. You've persevered through this challenge and no doubt made some significant changes in how you relate to and love your husband. Now it's time to celebrate!

Memory Verse

Do nothing out of selfish ambition or vain conceit. Rather, in humility value others above yourselves.

Philippians 2:3

Write this week's memory verse on a sticky note or index card and post it on your bathroom mirror or somewhere you'll see it often.

Bonus Week Two Challenges

This week, you'll be planning an overnight date for you and your husband to enjoy. Each day, you'll complete one portion of planning this fun date. I have also included suggestions for those of you who may be on a tight budget and/or can't leave the house.

I realize this may be difficult for parents of a newborn, or if you or your husband are struggling with illness, or taking care of aging parents. So please be sure to put your own twist on these challenges and make them work for your family, and the "An At-Home Alternative" section following Day Five has suggestions for those who simply can't get away. Browse the ideas and see if you can make even a little bit of fun happen. You both deserve it.

Day One

First things first. Pray over your trip. Ask God to guide your plans and pray for your relationship with your husband to be blessed. Pray also for safe travels and for God's will in every aspect of your trip.

Next, it's not very exciting, but you most likely need to plan a budget for your trip. If you're going to have to save up a little, estimate how much you can save from each paycheck and plan around that.

Set a reasonable amount, one your husband will likely agree with. If money is a hot-button issue in your home, check with him first.

Be sure to include the following in your budget:

- Transportation to your destination
- Transportation while there (if needed)
- Lodging
- Food
- A fun outing

- If you can spare it, include money to bring some romantic elements. (Sneak a peek at Day Four's challenge for more info.)

Ways to Find Funds

If you get cash from family on birthday or holidays, earmark that for your trip.

Stalk coupon sites like Groupon and Living Social to find great deals for both nearby destinations and those farther away.

Keep an envelope and add small amounts of cash to it over time. When you save money on something you always buy, put the amount you saved in the envelope. If you have cash on hand, take some out every now and then and add it to your envelope. I used to pilfer our grocery money, since we used cash for it. I would keep a five-dollar bill aside every time I went to the store and add it to the money I was saving to buy gifts for my husband. It really does add up.

Save gift cards that you receive and use them for the trip.

Sell something. Do you have stuff around the house you could sell? Hold a yard sale or sell it online. Facebook has tons of local buy-and-sell groups these days, and I've made a little bit of money from selling things we no longer needed.

Consider lower-cost lodging. With options like Airbnb, home exchange programs, RV rentals, or even camping, you can cut costs and still get away. Also look into any local retreat centers and see if they have rooms available overnight at a low rate. Don't be afraid to get on the phone and talk to someone onsite. Explain your situation, and they may be able to help you find a great deal.

Day Two

1. **Find a destination he'll love.** Since you're only going away for one night, you may want to stay within either driving distance or a quick flight so you don't spend all of your time traveling. Choose a place with his interests in mind. Does he

love the beach, or the lake, or a certain small town or big city nearby? Is there a forest or mountain you could visit? Get online and do some fun research. Tomorrow, you're going to find a fun outing in the area you choose. If you already have an outing in mind, then plan your destination around that.

2. **Reserve lodging.** Or at least make a more precise plan for when you'll do so, if you need to save up your funds first. Before you set your dates, you'll want to consider the following:

   • **Childcare.** If you have kids, now is the time to call the grandparents or your trusty babysitter. Or, offer to swap weekends with a friend and watch their kids so they can get away, too. If babysitting isn't possible, you can plan a trip with your kids or you can do an at-home date. You may have to tone down the romance a little, but it'll still be more fun than an ordinary day.

   • **Both of your work schedules.** A surprise trip could be fun, but if it's not possible due to scheduling or work responsibilities, tell him what you're planning and get the dates set together. If you have access to his work schedule, then plan your trip around his days off if possible.

   • **Clearing the calendar.** Besides work, make sure there are no appointments, school activities, or anything else that will conflict with your trip. Then, set your trip days aside and don't let anything else get scheduled on those days.

Day Three

1. **Plan a fun outing.** Choose something you'll both enjoy, but keep his interests especially in mind. Staying within your budget, research the destination and find something fun for the two of you to do during the day. Buy tickets or make

reservations if necessary. Try to keep most of the evening free, so you can have a romantic night in your room. Some ideas: Get a couples' massage, go to a concert or a sporting event, go canoeing or kayaking, or take a hike.

2. **Research where you'll be staying and find some restaurants to choose from.** If you're on a tight budget, check coupon sites again for local food at a bargain price. I like to plan all of our meals ahead of time. If you like a more laid-back approach, search a few options and make reservations if needed. Just remember to save a good portion of the evening to spend in your room. In fact, a romantic dinner in your hotel room might be perfect if your hotel has room service. And don't forget breakfast. A lazy breakfast in bed after a morning spent making love sounds blissful!

3. **Research transportation.** If you're in a big city with plans at certain times, you may want to check out the transportation options so you're not stressed out later.

Day Four

Prepare a night of romance. Make a list of things you'll need to gather and bring when the time comes to leave for the trip. Plan to spend most of the evening in your room, connecting emotionally and physically. Some romantic suggestions:

Yummy scented shower gel (that you can use together!)

Something silky to wear

Massage oil. Make sure you put it to use!

Romantic music to play

Perfume

Mints

Battery-operated candles. (You probably can't light real candles in a hotel room, so these would be a nice touch.)

If you're staying in a nice hotel, call ahead and order chocolate-covered strawberries and a sparkling drink to be delivered to the room. If you're driving to your destination, you can bring your own.

A warning: Don't put too much emphasis on having a sexy night if you've been having trouble in that area lately. Neither of you need the pressure. Instead of going all out with the romance, tone it down a little, have a nice dinner, and just see what happens. If you end the night snuggling, you've made progress.

Day Five #byhbonusdate

Invite your husband. You're ready to let your husband in on the secret! You can make him a sweet card and share the details, send him a video, or just tell him. Let him know you've got everything covered and that he's going to have the night of his life. (Hold off on this part if you're saving up for a few months. Take your time to plan things, and when you're ready, let him know.)

During the date. A few tips to make your time away great:

1. *Before you go, make sure you prepare yourself* so you feel most attractive, paying attention to things your husband would appreciate. Groom your bikini area, shave your legs, and moisturize your skin.

2. *Keep things light.* This isn't the time to address problems in your relationship. Even if you're in a marital rough spot, try to set those issues aside for twenty-four hours and just enjoy your husband. It will bless both of you if you can.

3. *Focus on him.* Put your phone away. Think about subjects he enjoys discussing. If you tend to be the talker, avoid subjects that don't excite him. (Hint: I will not be discussing home-school plans on this date!)

4. *Enjoy uninterrupted sex.* A hotel room probably is as private a space as you're going to get. Plan for and enjoy zero

interruptions. This means turning your phone off while you're enjoying each other. If worrying about being cut off from kids at home is going to stress you to the point of ruining your time, give your sitter the hotel information, with instructions to use only in an emergency. If there is a true emergency, they'll be able to reach you by calling your hotel room directly. Otherwise, shut out the rest of the world for a few hours! You'll both be better for it.

5. *Flirt all day.* Make eye contact, hold hands, pat his bottom, sit on the same side of the table when eating. Don't feel like you have to save sex for the evening. Have a quickie when you check in, wake him up with a surprise and intimately enjoy each other before breakfast, or take a long shower together.

An At-Home Alternative

What if you can't leave the house, can't leave the kids, or just can't get away for some reason? Plan an at-home overnight date.

1. **Clear the calendar.** Just as if you were whisking away to another city, block off a whole day, the night, and at least breakfast time on the second day. Make it work with all of your schedules and be firm about saying no to other things so you can make your special evening happen.

2. **Arrange for childcare if possible.** Can you have an older child watch the younger ones while you have dinner in your room?

   Or, put the kids to bed a little early and spend a couple hours connecting with your husband. Sure, you may be interrupted by a toddler with a bad dream, or a baby needing to nurse, but as long as you have good and flexible attitudes about it, you can still have a fun evening. Sometimes just acknowledging that this will likely happen beforehand helps everyone's attitudes stay pleasant.

3. **If you can manage a fun outing during the day, find something local to do.** No big deal if you have to pack up the kids and take them with you. You might not have a romantic time, but you'll have some great family time.

4. **Incorporate as many of the ideas from Day Four Challenges as you can.** Order meals to go from his favorite restaurant, or cook a special dinner. Shower together, slip into something slinky, and give him a massage by candlelight.

5. **Don't be discouraged that you can't get away.** Chances are, the season of life you're in will change soon enough, and you'll have plenty of opportunities to get away later on.

Getaway Date Planning Sheet

Our destination: _____

Share photos of your date and use #ourbonusdate and #blessyour husband

Our total budget	$_____
Transportation	$_____
Lodging	$_____
Food	$_____
Fun outing	$_____
Romantic goodies	$_____

Lodging at: _____

Confirmation #: _____

Dates: _____

Childcare arrangements: _____

Notes: _____

Nearby restaurants: _____

To do:

- ☐ Plan fun outing
- ☐ Purchase tickets or make reservations for fun outing if needed
- ☐ Plan dinner in your room if possible
- ☐ Order something sweet and something sparkly to drink, if possible
- ☐ Invite your husband

Romance boosters to pack:

- ☐ Something sexy to wear
- ☐ Scented shower gel
- ☐ Massage oil
- ☐ Romantic music
- ☐ Perfume
- ☐ Mints
- ☐ Electric candles

Day Two — Selfless with Our Time

Pray

Pray that God will reveal any changes you need to make in how you spend the time He gives you. Pray that you and your husband would honor God with how you choose to spend your time, and that you would have diligent hands and not be lazy.[1]

Meditate

As you look at your memory verse today, highlight or underline the verse in your Bible. Double underline or use a different color for: *consider others better than yourselves.*

Dwell

My husband always makes time for my _____.

Breathe

Since we're focusing on being selfless this week, let's start with one of our most precious commodities: time.

I actually think that most women are pretty selfless with their time. We give freely to everyone around us. If we have kids, they no doubt get most of our time. We give our time to work, to ministry, to our friends, to our parents, to those in need. Hopefully we're giving some time each day to God and His Word. And we do give time to our husbands, I don't doubt it.

So how can you be even more selfless in giving your time?

What Giving Your Time Looks Like

Giving time to your husband is going to look different for every marriage, and in every season. A new mom might be able to spare five minutes of talking time before bed each night. A retired wife might give up an afternoon yoga class to go on a walk with her husband.

Here are some ideas to choose from. Again, don't look at this as a must-do list. Think of it as a menu to choose from.

Time for leisure
Time to talk
Time to serve together
Time to pray together
Time to relax
Time for exercise
Time for sex
Time preparing for him
Time supporting his dreams

Evaluate Your Schedule

Do your activities leave you so busy that you don't have any time to give to your husband? I find myself in this situation too often. Every year—or more, if needed—I evaluate my schedule and decide if anything needs to be cut so that I have more time for what is important. I don't think I've ever evaluated my schedule and thought, *Huh. I did it! Nothing needs to go.* I have a very hyper personality and tend to take on too much. I usually start to notice that I need to scale back if I haven't had dinner with my husband in too many days.

Set aside some time to take stock of your commitments and see if anything needs to go.

Determine Your Priorities

We each have 1,440 minutes every day. Can you spare five minutes for your husband? Ten? Thirty? One full hour?

Don't compare yourself with other wives—do what works for you. If this is going to be a difficult change for you, start small.

Spend Ten Minutes Preparing

There is so much you could accomplish in ten short minutes when you put your mind to it. Occasionally, I will time myself doing a task that I've been putting off, and I'll find that it only takes me a couple of minutes. I try to remember that the next time I put it off. *It's only going to take two minutes,* I tell myself. *Just do it!*

What could you do in the ten minutes before you see your husband at the end of a workday? If you're home before your husband, here are a few things you could do in ten quick minutes. (If your husband is home before you, read on for more ideas.)

- Run a brush through your hair.

- Get dressed, if you haven't already.

- Pray that you'll be a blessing to him when he comes home.

- Put a smile on your face and determine to be pleasant. Withhold any issues that need to be discussed so that he can have a few minutes to decompress from his day.

- If you have little ones, get them excited for Daddy to come home.

- Pick up any clutter that he'll see as soon as he walks in the door.

I used to jump up and start doing the dishes when my husband got home, because I knew a sink full of dirty dishes drove him crazy. I quickly learned that the dishes didn't need to be done, as long as I was working on doing them. And my procrastinating self waited until I heard the garage door open every day. I admitted this once in a marriage workshop I was giving that my husband happened to be attending, and he told me he had known what I was up to for a while.

If your husband gets home before you every day, here are some ways you can prepare for him:

- Pray that you'll be a blessing to him when you see him.

- Freshen your breath so you can plant a big old kiss on him.

- Before you walk in the door, stop and take a couple of deep breaths. Put a smile on your face and determine to be pleasant. Leave the worries of the day behind if possible, or at least for the first few minutes.

If you completed a challenge today, list it here:

Day Three — Let Him Know You Need Him

Pray

Pray that you will be quick to listen, slow to speak, and slow to become angry. Pray that you would make wise plans by seeking advice.[2]

Meditate

Read this week's verse twice out loud, then attempt to say it without looking.

Dwell

I feel happy when my husband helps me _____.

Breathe

When I was getting started with the *Bless Your Husband* Daily Challenges Facebook Group, I asked my male friends for some ideas, both on Facebook and in person. I asked them, "What could your wife do that would bless you?" I was expecting lots of answers about the two things we're constantly told men care about: sex and food. And maybe a little respect thrown in there for good measure.

I was surprised when over and over, men said two things. Though they stated it in different ways, many of the responses boiled down to wanting to feel supported and needed.

Wait, what?

Even though I knew this in a logical sense, I was blown away that this was the knee-jerk response when men were asked how

174

their wives could bless them. They didn't want breakfast in bed and spontaneous sex? Okay, some of them did.

But more of them focused on their feelings. Shocking, right?

For today, we're going to focus on their need to feel needed. Do you think your husband feels that you need him?

I'm reminded of an episode of *The Andy Griffith Show*. Aunt Bea—a lovable character who takes care of her widower nephew, Andy, and his adorable son, Opie—has to leave town. Andy and Opie decide they'll surprise Aunt Bea and take care of everything that needs doing and clean the house before she comes home. After much sitcom hilarity ensues, Andy quickly realizes that Aunt Bea needs to feel needed. And it's not until they deliberately make a mess again and she has to clean it up that she's back to feeling like her happy self.

While it's easy to see that a nurturing aunt would want to feel needed, it's a little harder to see our husbands in this light.

Would you agree that, even if your husband wouldn't say it, on some level he, too, needs to be needed? Is there something you can do to show him that you need him?

Ask for His Advice (and Take It)

In the beginning of our marriage, I was pretty headstrong about being independent and making my own decisions. Then, when I was at church and would hear about how the husband is to be the spiritual leader of the home, I would be silently disappointed. Why wasn't my husband the leader he was supposed to be?

It wasn't too long before I realized that the biggest stumbling block for my husband was his stubborn wife. Little by little, I started running things by my husband, and little by little, my trust in him grew as he became the leader of our home. Before long, I was trusting him to make major decisions for us. And as hard as that can be at times, there is so much more freedom in that.

It was also scary. Until I learned that we have the biggest safety net ever.

As I grew in my trust of Eric, I was learning to trust God. My husband has failed, and he will fail again, and yours will, too. But if you trust that God is going to be there for you and make good of it, no matter what happens, you can take that leap of faith, knowing for certain you'll be caught.

If you're not ready to trust your husband with something big, start small by asking his advice on little things. Just be sure you're willing to follow through and take his advice.

Ask your husband what you should cook for your next dinner party, or which dress you should wear for church. That's not exactly going to make him feel needed, but it's a good start. In time, make an effort to build up to bigger things. How should you handle the note from your child's teacher, or what church should you attend? Asking for his advice in this way isn't to manipulate your man into feeling wise or special. It's a choice to honor him.

Ask for Help

Oh, this is a hard one for me. Even though I know better, to this day it is still difficult for me to ask my husband for help. I can even get sassy when he tries to help me. In fact, I recently did one of those Facebook quizzes where you ask your husband a list of questions and post his answers. One of the questions I had to ask him was "How do I annoy you?" His reply: "When I try to do something for you and you say, 'I didn't ask for your help.'"

Guilty! I assume this goes back to my old stubborn, independent ways of my youth. You know that phase toddlers go through when they don't want you putting their shoes on or doing anything else for them because they've learned to do it on their own? Well, I guess I never grew out of that.

But asking for help is such a simple way to make our husbands feel needed and useful. I've had to humble myself more and more as I live with chronic pain, so I have gotten better at this lately, mostly because I've had no choice. But I have to admit, it still bothers me. (I almost feel that I can't even really tell you to ask for your husband's help since I'm so lousy about doing it.) So let's all just agree to try to be better about asking for help.

I'm not saying we should be helpless, or act like damsels in distress. I think being strong and independent is more attractive (not to mention more authentic) than being helpless. But I also want Eric to feel like a big strong man who gets to rescue me once in a while, because the truth is, he has rescued me in many ways. And he deserves that spot in my life.

Okay, I talked myself into it. How about you?

If you completed a challenge today, list it here:

_____

_____

Be the One Who Is Interested in Your Husband

Day Four

Pray

Pray that you would love your husband the way Jesus loves you and that he'll feel accepted and cared for at home.[3]

Meditate

Copy this week's memory verse here:

_____

_____

_____

Dwell

My husband likes to talk about _____ more than anything.

Breathe

Doesn't it feel good when someone is interested in you? As introverted as I am, I still feel special when a friend remembers something about me and asks me for updates when I see them. And if it's my husband who is interested, even better.

I think I'm a little quirky in that I *really* need to feel my husband is interested in my life. We're so different that he's not actually interested in most of the things that consume my time: homeschooling, writing, and reading. So I've gotten really good about telling him that I need to tell him my homeschool plans, and he needs to at least listen a little. And he's gotten really good about not falling asleep while I'm talking.

Maybe not everyone feels this need so keenly—after all, I am a middle child—but I would venture to guess that the majority of us would like someone to take an interest in our day and life.

That includes our husbands.

As much as I am able to recognize and verbalize my need to be interesting, I know that on some level, my husband has the same need. And so does yours.

I don't think the problem with most of us is that we're uninterested, or don't love our husbands enough to care. I think the problem is that we get busy, life gets hectic or into a rut, and the routines of everyday life take over without our realizing it.

Instead of lingering over a conversation with our husbands, we're trying to get dinner on the table and get to baseball practice and just get some sleep already.

Just a few intentional choices will help you get interested in your husband again.

Ways to Show You Are Interested

1. **Try to remember what he has going on in his day.** After twenty years together, I still don't understand a lot of my husband's work. Sometimes my eyes glaze over when he's talking numbers, just as his do when I want to discuss the latest writing lesson I taught. But I try to remember key phrases and the overall idea of what he's talking about, so I can follow up with him about it later. A simple, "How did that appointment go?" the next day shows him you care. Or, send a text and let him know you're praying for him when he has a big meeting.

2. **Inquire about his hobbies.** Learn a little about what he is into. No need to become a super fan, but learn enough to have an intelligent conversation with him about it.

3. **Listen attentively.** This means putting the phone down, making eye contact, and absorbing what he's saying. Avoid the temptation to interrupt him, but don't be afraid to ask him to wait for a second so you can tie something up and give him your full attention. Eric sometimes bursts into the room already talking, and as much as I'd love to say I'm the wife who literally drops everything for him, I usually need a second to switch my focus.

4. **Become attuned to his needs.** Sometimes, my husband will be venting about a relationship or other issue, and I am quick to offer advice on how he should handle the situation. Of course, what he usually wants is for me to just listen. There are times that giving advice is appropriate, and there are times when it's not helpful. Learn the difference. Being quick to listen and slow to speak (as we're admonished to in James 1:19) is one of my all-time great challenges, but with God's help it is possible.

5. **Be happy to see him!** Light up when he walks in the room. Smile. Give him a kiss.

6. **Don't push too hard.** If your husband is not a big talker, you'll just have to listen more carefully. Don't stress him out by trying to pry him open so that you can be more interested in him. Accept him for who he is and delight in the things he does share.

Remember, we're choosing selflessness this week. Put your need to be heard aside and listen to your husband.

And the fact is, someone, somewhere *is* going to be interested in your husband. Wouldn't you like it to be you?

If you completed a challenge today, list it here:

_____

_____

Day Five	Final Thoughts

Pray

Pray that God will give you strength and uphold you with His righteous right hand as you move forward and continue to love and bless your husband.[4]

Meditate

Write this week's memory verse from memory:

_____

_____

_____

Dwell

I am proud of myself for learning to

_____

_____

_____

Breathe

This week, we've covered being selfless with our time, our egos (asking for his advice and help), and our attention (being interested in him).

But really, we've covered so much more than that. Everything about the challenges throughout this book goes back to your being selfless. You've chosen, little by little, to think of your husband first. To focus on his needs, not your own. In a world of me, me, me, you've chosen him.

If I could encourage you in any one thing as we wrap up this challenge and you move forward with your married life, it would be this:

Keep choosing him.

You're going to get tired of it. You're going to get annoyed. You're going to feel taken advantage of. You're going to pick up a magazine at the salon and read an article about how he's not meeting your needs, and you're going to get irritated. You're going to have friends telling you to put yourself first.

And sometimes, you will. You'll get out of the habits you've made, and you'll get a little cranky. It happens to all of us.

So when that happens—not if, but when—cut yourself some slack. Remember that we're not doing these things to earn favor, and that not doing these things doesn't make us a bad wife. Keep in mind that we are not defined by what we do.

Remember the verses you've memorized and the goals you've met. Go back and read your "dwell" statements and some of your journaling. Remind yourself of your strengths and how far you've come. As much as I love passing books on, this is one book I hope you'll keep and refer back to for years to come. Not for the words I've written here, but for the words you've written.

If you completed a challenge today, list it here:

_____

_____

Weekend Reflection

How can you make more time for your husband?

_____

_____

_____

_____

On the Day Two list of ways to give your time, which item do you make the most time for when it comes to your husband? The least?

_____

_____

_____

Do you think your husband feels needed by you?

_____

_____

In what ways can you work on showing more interest in your husband?

_____

_____

When you've had a chance to have your date, come back and write about it here.

_____

_____

_____

Congratulations

You did it! You persevered and completed six whole weeks (or more) and you rocked your marriage. Thank you for taking this journey with me.

I'm so proud of you.

If you've reached this point and finished the whole thing, won't you please drop me an email? I'd like to send a little bonus just for you. And don't worry, you won't end up on some annoying mailing list. This is a one-time email, no strings attached. Email me at ifinished@angelamillsbooks.com.

May your marriage be blessed!

Resources

Using *Bless Your Husband* in a Group Setting

Are you part of a weekly Bible study group, moms' group, or marriage group? Or are you thinking of starting a group of like-minded wives? This six-week challenge could provide some great material.

Blessing your husband with the support of a group offers:

Accountability. Who among us doesn't need a little accountability to stay on track? I'm much more likely to finish something if I know I'm going to meet up with others.

Prayer support. Wouldn't it be wonderful to have wives praying for each other as you work through the challenge?

Varied perspectives. Soak in the wisdom of women who are further along in their journey than you are or who have walked down a path that is new to you in your marriage.

Encouragement. You can each share wisdom and encouragement. Someone may need to hear your thoughts and stories!

Camaraderie. Two are better than one, and three are better than two. You can even plan some couples' nights out. When my husband and I were part of a marriage Bible study small group, we had several fun group dates, and even went on two retreats together.

Sample Routines for Meetings

1. You may want to start or end with mingling time, maybe with beverages or a snack, depending on your group. This social time can benefit those who are looking for new friends and deeper connections. Setting this time aside at the beginning gives latecomers a chance to arrive before the discussion starts.

2. Open in prayer. Set a firm starting time, and gather everyone to open in prayer.

3. Say the week's memory verse as a group. Don't worry if you haven't memorized it yet and need to read along in your Bible. God's Word being spoken is always a good thing!

4. Discussion: Use the Weekend Reflection each week to guide your discussions. You may also want to check in with each other on the tasks and discuss which you enjoyed most/least that week. You could discuss your weekly goals, too, if time permits.

5. Share prayer requests, then close in prayer. Depending on the size of your group, you may break into smaller groups for this.

Keep It Positive

1. Commit to making the group discussions and prayer time about how you can improve as wives, not about how your husbands need to improve. You may want to give a friendly reminder at the start of each meeting.

   If someone continually complains about her husband, the leader can privately and gently remind her of what the focus is to be. Rest assured, this is something most wives struggle with from time to time. But if the group as a whole chooses not to complain about their husbands, it is possible to keep the meetings positive, and God will bless your efforts.

2. Avoid comparisons. Each member of the group could be tempted to compare herself and her husband to other couples. What comes easily to one wife might be more difficult for you. How another husband responds to something may be drastically different from how yours responds. An extrovert who is expressive may find it easier to show his appreciation, while a more reserved, quiet type may keep his appreciation inside.

And let's not forget that plenty of husbands won't even notice when half of these challenges are done . . . and that's okay! Remember, the point is to grow as a wife. Try to focus on the good things God has given you. But if you're struggling with comparison, be honest and ask for prayer.

Online Materials

Group leaders will find extra discussion questions, media resources, printables, more ideas, and information just for them on my website at angelamillsbooks.com/groupleaders.

Ideas for Busy Wives

Not every wife is going to be able to fully devote the time to do the *Bless Your Husband* challenge every day, so I've come up with a few ideas for those of you who are super busy.

Work in Smaller Chunks

Set a timer and commit to spending even five minutes a day. It's hard to talk yourself out of doing anything for just five minutes a day, isn't it? You won't make it through the book in six weeks, but that's okay! You'll still be growing as a wife and you will see changes because of it.

Write It on Your Schedule

Maybe you can add your daily reading time to your schedule at a certain time every day, and try to keep it like any other appointment. Then, when you finish this book, you'll have that time set aside for continued study or spiritual growth.

Work for Longer Periods

Maybe it would work better for you to set aside an hour every Saturday, and read through a few days at once. Doing a little every day would be ideal, but this solution is better than not doing anything at all.

Be Creative with Your Time

Do you have time during a coffee break at work you could use?

Leave a little early and work in your car for ten minutes before going in to work.

Wake up before your kids. This isn't always possible, I know. Sleep is important to keep you healthy and sane. But if you can spare a few minutes before anyone gets up, that might make it easier on you.

Can you lie on the floor and do your study while your toddler plays with blocks?

As my kids got older, I would often do my Bible study while they were doing schoolwork. As a homeschool mom, I had to find those little moments when my kids were busy and I wasn't teaching or doing laundry. It wasn't easy, but those years flew by, and I never regretted the time I spent nurturing my own spiritual growth.

Show Yourself Grace

If you get behind for a few days, or weeks, don't feel like you've failed. I have started and abandoned many studies, but it was when

I learned to give myself grace and say, "Late is better than never," that I was able to go back and finish what I had started.

If Your Marriage Is in Crisis

Some of you are battling such serious issues in your marriage that doing these challenges takes great strength to fight through the bitterness you're feeling. *What about me? Why doesn't he ever care enough to do things like this? Why should I be the one doing all the work? He doesn't even deserve this.*

Trust me, friend. I have thought all these things before. My husband does not have the same gift for expressing his love as I do. Elaborate endeavors aren't his thing, and his take on making an effort looks a lot different than mine does.

I don't want to share his failings here, or his big mistakes, because that's not my story to tell. Only my failings belong to me, and only my mistakes. But rest assured, I didn't marry a perfect man, and those stories do exist. You just won't read about them here.

I want to protect my husband in the same way I'd like him to protect me if he wrote a book on marriage. Talking about my own failings is one thing, but someone else talking about them—no thanks! But at the same time, I don't want you reading this book and thinking, *Sure, easy for her to say! She married a prince!*

Because while I did marry my prince, our road to happily ever after has been long and bumpy, and sometimes downright miserable. We're talking storms and motion sickness and wanting to drive right off a cliff.

So. If you're on a particularly crummy part of road right now, how do you keep going? How do you keep doing these challenges and holding on and being pleasant and baking cookies, for goodness' sake? What is that really going to do for your marriage when you can barely stand to be in the same room with him?

I mean, no one would blame you if you just gave up. If you just gave back to him what he so clearly deserves. If you chucked this book and chucked your marriage. If you wrote this crazy author and told her, "Hey, not everyone lives in a fairy tale, and she can take her cookies and . . ."

Sorry, I got a little carried away there.

My point is, I get it. I've been there. I've been crumpled up on the bathroom floor, sobbing and feeling hopeless. I've been on the internet at two a.m. searching for an apartment and a job, dreaming of a different life. I've been the one wandering around a department store because I didn't want to go home. I've. Been. There.

If this is you now, please hang in there. Modify the challenges if you need to. Have you ever done a workout video and seen the person off to the side, modifying the exercises for those with a bad back or bum knees? Well, take the same approach to the challenges. If you and your husband can barely talk to each other without it erupting into a fight, leave notes instead of starting conversations. If things are too tense to initiate sex, a hug might be enough. If you can't bake cookies without bitterness in your heart, buy him a candy bar instead.

Tread lightly, but don't let your problems stop you from showing love, even when he doesn't deserve it. As you work through the daily readings and challenges, I have no doubt that your heart will begin to change. What you're doing throughout this book is basically what I did to become a better wife and help get our marriage back on track.

But I didn't do it alone. Early on, we were blessed with an awesome marriage group that taught us much and held us accountable. I highly encourage you to find a Bible study for married couples as soon as possible. If your church doesn't offer one, try a larger church in your area.

If your problems are so difficult that you don't know if your marriage is going to make it, consider finding a marriage counselor. Many churches offer this service for free or at a low cost. It might just save your marriage, and that is always worth the time and effort.

This is where I have to stop and say, if you or your children are being abused, the time to separate is now. Find a trusted counselor or pastor and get help removing yourselves from the situation. Tell a friend, call the police, or go stay with your parents for a while. Just find a way to get out of there and then you can take the steps to see if the marriage can or should be saved.

And know that you are never alone. God is with you in this, and there are people who will help you, too. If you don't have friends or family you can trust, please call the National Domestic Violence Hotline at 1–800–799–7233, and they will help you figure out what to do. You can also go to their website at www. thehotline.org for a live chat and more information, but if you fear your internet use is being monitored, use the phone number provided.

Above all, know that God has not forgotten you. "He heals the brokenhearted and binds up their wounds" (Psalm 147:3).

Tips for Wives on a Tight Budget

It is my desire that none of the challenges in this book be unreachable for financial reasons alone. Nothing suggested here should put you in debt or cause strain on your marriage because you spent money that was needed for something else.

I have spent most of my adult life on a pretty tight budget. At first, my husband and I were young and just getting started with our careers, while paying for school and supporting the kids we already had. Then, our kids got older and we became a one-income, homeschooling family for many years. Let's just say I'm used to being broke. We've often lived paycheck to paycheck, and it wasn't always easy or fun. But it did make me very creative.

If you haven't yet, make sure you read "Content with Our Means" on page 146. This will help get your heart and mind in the right place. Now, on to the practical ideas!

Date Nights on a Budget

Planning dates when you're on a strict budget can cause added stress that neither of you needs. Can you add $4–$5 to an envelope each time you get paid and set it aside for dates? You can save up for an expensive night out, or you can do something low cost, and be able to go out more often.

Go out for ice cream at a fast-food place.
Rent a movie and make popcorn at home.
Browse a bookstore and go out for coffee.
Visit yard sales together.
Go fishing.
Go for a walk in a pretty part of town.
Go for a scenic drive.
Take Buzzfeed quizzes together online and laugh at your results.

Gift Giving on a Budget

Gift giving is already so complicated. Being on a tight budget makes it even more so. But some of the best gifts I've given and received came from creativity that we had to use because money was short.

Make your gifts. Homemade gifts are my favorite kind to receive. Pinterest offers a wealth of ideas.

Give experiences. Search those coupon sites again and find low-cost experiences to give to your husband as gift cards or certificates.

Be thoughtful. A small gift that reminds him of your first date will be remembered more fondly than a fancy watch.

Cooking on a Budget

When it's time to make your husband's favorite treats or meals and you don't have money for ingredients, get creative. If he loves filet mignon, get cube steak and serve it with a baked potato for the same feeling. Instead of an expensive cake made with European chocolate, buy an inexpensive cake mix and the house will smell just as good.

Buy pricey foods in smaller portions; you can still have special treats, just less or fewer of them.

Save a little grocery money each week until you can splurge and have one special dinner every other month or so.

Check grocery sales and keep an eye out for treats he likes that you usually can't afford. Or, check the clearance area of your grocery store. I remember finding gourmet pastries on sale, very cheap since they were about to expire, and bringing them home for that night's dessert. It was an unusual treat for us back then, and we were all excited.

Memorizing Scripture[1]

A couple of years ago, I was leading a Bible study group for young girls. I assigned them a verse each week to memorize. We wrote them on index cards, recited them together, and learned their meaning. Without fail, every week the girls would return and say they just couldn't remember it. It was too hard!

One evening the girls arrived, and I told them we were going to play a game. We all sat in a circle, and each girl thought of a favorite song, and said just the first line. Anyone who knew it started singing along. Song after song, the girls chimed in. They knew them all! We laughed and sang, and remembered "old" songs from when they were younger.

Once everyone settled down, I kindly pointed out that they had memorized those songs without even trying. How? Well, they answered, because they liked them and heard them all the time. *Hmm.* Why is it you say it is impossible to memorize Scripture, I asked. As they began to get what I was saying, one by one they started to bite their lips, avoid my eyes, and thumb through their Bibles.

I hadn't meant to lay a guilt trip on them, yet that's exactly what I had done. But you know what? It worked. We brainstormed ways to memorize Scripture, and I encouraged the girls to recite their verse at least once a day.

The next week, every single one of them had memorized a verse.

The funny thing is, I had been in similar groups with some of these girls' moms and many of them said the same thing about memorizing Bible verses. "It's just too hard!" I have heard so many women say this, and I myself have been lax at times out of laziness.

There are so many reasons to practice memorizing God's Word. I will share just a few here. But first, abolish all excuses.

Memorizing Scripture Is Not Hard

Think about all we've memorized in our lifetime:

- Songs
- Speeches from history
- Poems
- Excerpts from plays
- Funny lines from movies
- The Pledge of Allegiance
- Bank account numbers
- Social security and driver's license numbers
- Important dates

Now that we're biting our lips and looking shiftily around the room, read on for some reasons to inspire you.

God Says So

Yep. Just look:

Fix these words of mine in your hearts and minds; tie them as symbols on your hands and bind them on your foreheads. Teach them to your children, talking about them when you sit at home and when you walk along the road, when you lie down and when you get up. Write them on the doorframes of your houses and on your gates, so that your days and the days of your children may be many in the land that the LORD swore to give your forefathers, as many as the days that the heavens are above the earth.

Deuteronomy 11:18–21

Who can argue with that? God commands us in this, as in all things, for our own good!

Memorizing Scripture Helps Keep You from Sinning

Psalm 119:11: "I have hidden your word in my heart, that I might not sin against you."

In Matthew 4:1–11, Jesus quoted Scripture to Satan when He was being tempted in the wilderness. Satan was actually distorting the Scriptures, and Jesus set him straight with God's Word. Don't you want to make sure you can stand against the devil's schemes? I know I do!

In Ephesians 6:17, when Paul is talking about standing firm against the devil, he tells us that the Word of God is the sword of the Spirit. Use it!

Memorizing Scripture Helps You Encourage Others

"Let the word of Christ dwell in you richly as you teach and admonish one another with all wisdom, and as you sing psalms, hymns and spiritual songs with gratitude in your hearts to God" (Colossians 3:16).

Jesus said, "Out of the overflow of the heart, the mouth speaks" (Matthew 12:34 BSB).

How awesome is it when you are sharing a problem with a friend and they give you the perfect Scripture? I know God has used many women to speak His Word to me when I needed it, and I strive to be that kind of friend to others.

What kind of friend, wife, and mom will you be? Will you give flippant advice based on feelings, or reach out to others with God's healing Word?

Memorizing Scripture Trains Your Mind

"Do not conform to the pattern of this world, but be transformed by the renewing of your mind. Then you will be able to test and approve what God's will is—his good, pleasing and perfect will" (Romans 12:2).

How do we renew our mind? Philippians 4:8 gives us a clue: "Finally, brothers and sisters, whatever is true, whatever is noble, whatever is right, whatever is pure, whatever is lovely, whatever is admirable—if anything is excellent or praiseworthy—think about such things."

How do we know what is true, noble, and right? There is only one source that tells us for sure and that is the Bible.

Keeping God's Word in your mind and heart will keep your mind on heavenly things.

Here Are Ten Tips to Help You Memorize Scripture

1. Stick a Post-it on your bathroom mirror, nightstand, desk, or fridge—anywhere you'll see it often.
2. Keep an index card with the verse on it in your purse or wallet and refer to it during the day.
3. Put a Scripture on a note in your phone, take a screenshot of it, and keep it as your lock screen. You'll see it every time you check your phone for the time during the day.

4. Recite the verse out loud to yourself several times. If you have kids, have them join in, too.

5. Try to find the verse set to music. Many are available on YouTube for free. I found one just by typing "Philippians 4:8 song" into the search bar on YouTube.

6. Make up your own song.

7. Pray the verse over yourself, your family, and anyone else who may need it.

8. Set the alarm on your phone with the verse as the label.

9. Write the verse out by hand.

10. Try a Bible verse memory app. My favorite is Scripture Typer.

Online Content

All readers are welcome to download from my website additional content to go along with this book. At the time of this writing, these bonuses include:

- A downloadable video of my workshop, "A Wife to Rush Home To"
- Six printable Scripture cards, one for each memory verse in this book
- Five printable notecards for you to color for your husband, designed with guided words of encouragement and gratitude
- Printable homemaking lists and helps
- Meal planning helps

To download your content, go to angelamillsbooks.com/husband bonuscontent and enter the password *wifey* to gain access.

Acknowledgments

It all started with the proposal! To my agent, Janet Kobobel Grant, for working hard to polish my proposal and making it a great one. Thank you for believing in me and for plucking this idea out of the dozens of others and knowing it was The One. I'm so blessed to have an agent whom I trust implicitly. Your guidance is priceless.

To my editor, Kim Bangs, for saying I do! Thank you for making this book happen and for guiding me through the process with kindness and patience.

To editor Sharon Hodge: your expertise, insightful comments, and questions that made me dig deeper made editing this book such a pleasant process. Thanks for making this book the best it could be!

To my husband, Eric, who supports and encourages me and lets me put our imperfect marriage on display so that others might benefit from hearing what God has done in our life. And thanks, too, for choosing me that night. I'm glad we waited for the third Eric.

To my daughter Chloe, who has always told me that I need to write books, and who made dinners many nights when she was a teenager so that I could write, write, write. I love your deep strength and unwavering faith. Your dedication to being a godly wife is inspiring!

To my daughter Sophie, who prayed and prayed for this dream of mine to come true and who sweetly nagged me about making sure I finished on time. I love your passion for life and your soft and generous heart. Your joyful spirit makes every day better!

To my son-in-law, Christopher, for being the kind of husband parents dream their daughter will one day have.

To my mom, Kathleen Carlisle, my first friend, my first reader, my first fan, and my constant encourager. Thank you for modeling a marriage that actually looks fun in a world that tries to make it look burdensome, and for teaching me to be real.

To my dad, Greg Chamberlin, for buying me my first word processor and for truly supporting me in every way. Thank you for your unfailing generosity, for raising me to be strong and independent, and for setting the bar so high for what a man is supposed to be.

To my second mom, Debby Chamberlin, who has advised me and encouraged me without fail and who has been an amazing wife to my dad and a powerful, godly example to me. I'm so glad God answered my prayers and made you my second mom!

To my second dad, Randy Carlisle, for scaring all of my boyfriends, but accepting my husband as one of your own, and for being a strong and constant presence in my life.

To my mother-in-law, Carol Mills, for raising an incredible man, for supporting us in so many ways, for your overwhelming generosity, and for accepting your son's goofy wife.

To my Aunt Diana, who gave me the advice that I most often quote. You told me to make sure I stayed friends with my husband, and I took it to heart. Thank you for setting my priorities straight, way back when Sophie was a baby.

To Jacob and Destiny, for being the most beautiful example of a biblical marriage that most of us have ever seen. I love you and appreciate you more than you know.

To my anonymous friend, who secretly provided for me to go to a writer's conference, where this journey would begin. I'm so thankful for your generosity and belief in me. Look what God did with that gift! I promise I will pay it forward.

To more loved ones for their love and support: Seth, Brent, Jake, Radiance, Tim, Brianna, Aunt Nancy, Mike and Janie, Uncle Ron, Scott and Kat, Andrea and Dominic, Grandmas Mable and

Irma, and of course our little Jude for making his Grannie smile every day.

To Gary Little, for teaching Eric and me so much in those early days. Your generosity and wise guidance changed us for the better and I'll never forget it.

To authors Bill and Pam Farrel for your encouragement and advice. I value it highly! Thank you for going out of your way to meet Eric and me and speak into our lives.

To my beautiful prayer team, with many thanks for covering me in prayer throughout this process. Your prayers are priceless to me: Eric Bishop, Kelly Duran, Kathy Giordano, Michelle Smith, Mom, and Debby.

To the women in the *Bless Your Husband* Daily Challenges Facebook Group. Your honesty, kindness, and desire to bless your husbands inspire me every day. Thank you for taking this journey with me!

To my faithful and loving God, Father, and Savior. Thank you for all the reminders that your grace is enough. To God be the glory.

Notes

Foreword

1. Bill and Pam Farrel, *The 10 Best Decisions a Single Can Make: Embracing All God Has for You* (Eugene, OR: Harvest House, 2011), 64.
2. 1619. Ektenós, *Strong's Concordance* and HELPS Word-studies, http://biblehub.com/greek/1619.htm.

Week One: The Wife of His Youth

1. Romans 12:2
2. Psalm 146:2
3. 1 Corinthians 10:13; Psalm 19:14
4. Ephesians 4:12

Week Two: The Servant Wife

1. Philippians 2:13
2. Elizabeth George, *A Woman after God's Own Heart* (Eugene, OR: Harvest House, 2006), 275. Though not stated as such, George's writing on this could be a paraphrase of German philosopher Arthur Schopenhauer's "Each day is a little life: every waking and rising a little birth, every fresh morning a little youth, every going to rest and sleep a little death," from *Counsels and Maxims, The Essays of Arthur Schopenhauer* (South Australia: The University of Adelaide), ebook.
3. Genesis 2:18; Proverbs 17:22
4. Philippians 2:3–5; Philippians 4:13
5. Ephesians 4:15; Philippians 4:19

Week Three: The Barnabas Wife

1. Luke 12:12
2. Colossians 3:2; Romans 12:2
3. Hebrews 4:12; Psalm 1:2
4. Matthew 7:12; 1 Corinthians 15:33; Colossians 4:6

Week Four: The Beautiful Wife

1. Proverbs 31:30; 1 Peter 3:4
2. Romans 12:6

3. Galatians 6:4; 1 Thessalonians 5:16; Proverbs 17:22
4. Galatians 5:16; Proverbs 3:6

Bonus Week One: Cultivating Contentment While Making Your Home a Haven

1. Margaret Kim Peterson, *Keeping House: The Litany of Everyday Life* (San Francisco: Jossey-Bass, 2007), 107.
2. 1 Timothy 6:8; Philippians 4:8
3. George Lewis, "Are ya kidding me?! No complaints for 21 days," Today, March 5, 2007, https://www.today.com/news/are-ya-kidding-me-no-complaints -21-days-wbna17362505.
4. Will Bowen, About, http://willbowen.com.
5. Philippians 4:11, 13
6. 1 Peter 4:10; 1 Timothy 6:10; Hebrews 13:5
7. Proverbs 14:1; 31:21–27
8. Meik Wiking, *The Little Book of Hygge: Danish Secrets to Happy Living* (New York: Harper Collins, 2017), vi.

Bonus Week Two: Choosing Selflessness While Planning an Overnight Date

1. Psalm 90:12; Proverbs 10:4
2. James 1:19; Proverbs 12:15
3. John 13:34
4. Isaiah 41:10

Resources

1. This material was originally published as a blog post, Memorizing Scripture, You Can! February 4, 2010, www.angelamillsbooks.com/faith-2/following-jesus /memorizing-scripture-you-can/1550.

Angela Mills began blogging in 2008 and has written more than sixty articles for various magazines and websites. In addition to her blog, she runs a private Facebook group for thousands of Christian wives. She's been married to her best friend, Eric, for eighteen years and is a homeschool mom and proud grandma. Angela and her family live in Southern California with their dog, Lucy McGillicuddy Ricardo Mills.